BACKSTAGE PASS

BACKSTAGE PASS

TALES FROM BEYOND THE SQUARED CIRCLE

DAVID SAHADI

Published by ECW Press
665 Gerrard Street East
Toronto, Ontario, Canada M4M 1Y2
416-694-3348 / info@ecwpress.com

Editor for the Press: Michael Holmes
Copy editor: David Marsh
Cover designer: Jess Albert
Cover Image: Stephanie Koop
Images with Stone Cold and The Undertaker: Courtesy of Tom Buchanan
All remaining images are from the author's personal collection

LIBRARY AND ARCHIVES CANADA CATALOGUING IN PUBLICATION

Title: Backstage pass : tales from beyond the squared circle / David Sahadi.

Names: Sahadi, David, author.

Identifiers: Canadiana (print) 2025032072X | Canadiana (ebook) 20250320738

ISBN 978-1-77041-821-9 (softcover)
ISBN 978-1-77852-532-2 (PDF)
ISBN 978-1-77852-531-5 (ePub)

Subjects: LCSH: World Wrestling Entertainment, Inc. | LCSH: Wrestling—United States.

Classification: LCC GV1198.12 .S24 2026 | DDC 796.8120973—dc23

PRINTED AND BOUND IN CANADA

PRINTING: MARQUIS 5 4 3 2 1

This book is dedicated to a fellow author — my father,
Poppa Lou. Elias Joseph Sahadi was the greatest father one
could ever have, and the most loving man that ever lived.
With gentle guidance and a heart of love, my father
made me the man I am today. And I love him so . . .

CONTENTS

FOREWORD

David Sahadi doesn't need professional wrestling.

Professional wrestling needs David Sahadi.

Much like Hollywood, the grappling game gets more than its fair share of backstabbing, politicking and conniving from those trying to grab the proverbial brass ring. Match outcomes may be predetermined, but the ugliness that can unfold behind the scenes in the quest for stardom is very real. The industry's competitive nature breeds these me-first byproducts.

That's why someone as selfless as David should be revered and celebrated.

For more than twenty years, David has helped others look good without ever seeking the spotlight himself. I know this firsthand. Before becoming part of the business myself at All Elite Wrestling, I wrote about David's impact in the early 2000s in my syndicated weekly pro wrestling column at the South Florida *Sun Sentinel*.

David's passion, creativity and work ethic — all traits that would allow him to thrive in another line of work — have made him not only one of pro wrestling's top producers and directors, but a beacon of positivity in a genre that needs more of them.

I know that David's late father, Lou, was extremely proud of the man his son has become. *Backstage Pass: Tales from Beyond the Squared Circle* explains some of the reasons why, while also pulling back the curtain on some of pro wrestling's most memorable moments, told through David's unique perspective.

When you're done reading this book, you'll understand exactly why David is so revered by those he has worked with.

— ALEX MARVEZ, ALL ELITE WRESTLING

PREFACE

Professional wrestling is often a paradox. Storylines between combatants are intricately scripted by creative writers, refined by the wrestlers and their assigned agents on the day of the match, and performed live in front of a raucous crowd and worldwide television audience in an attempt to create drama and emotion.

It's scripted. It's "fake."

Yet, more often than not, it is the real-life machinations that happen backstage — behind-the-scenes tales of drama and deceit, pettiness between allies and adversaries — that feel as though they were written by Hollywood's finest scriptwriters. But they are not. At times the illusion of what happens inside the squared circle feels more real than what goes on out of the public eye, such as in company boardrooms. Yet the stories I witnessed and tell in this book are true.

Ken Anderson, a two-time TNA World Heavyweight Champion, had a motto that sold many T-shirts: "Wrestling Is Real. People Are Fake." In the world of professional wrestling, that truly describes it all.

Professional wrestling is a world of factions, secret coalitions and covert liaisons — all at odds with each other. All wanting to diminish and then defeat any threat to their power. And I'm talking about what happens backstage, not inside the ring.

In a world where politics is deeply entwined in the fabric of the business, I was different. I was a rare babyface in a world of heels. I solely cared about things that helped the product and the boss I was working for. Nothing else. And I still take great pride in trying to uplift and inspire people, whether they be crew members or young, emerging wrestlers, and in never diminishing someone's dreams. I'm the eternal optimist, the one who always sees the glass as half full.

Terry Taylor once told me a parable.

"David, there are two ways to have the tallest building in town," he said. "One is to build it; the other is to tear down all of the taller buildings around you."

From an early age, I chose to be a builder. I learned that from my beloved father.

What you are about to read are real-life stories that are often more compelling and dramatic than what happens inside the ring. They are glorious, nefarious, heartbreaking, and at times truly unbelievable. Mega-matches behind the scenes between the powers that ruled, those who desired to do so, and the leaders and decision-makers who were often in agreement but mostly at odds. Professional wrestling is a business where it's hard to know who to trust. Betrayal comes in many unforeseen forms.

"Wrestling Is Real. People Are Fake."

In ways most don't know, that says it all.

1

NBC SPORTS

I never learned a thing in high school. Or college. School taught me nothing I needed to know about life. Life, however, taught me everything I needed to know about . . . everything.

Although I graduated with a BA in mathematics, my first job was in construction, working for a local millionaire who took advantage of a young man without a job and without a plan. And I hated math.

Without a map to follow, I was rudderless, drifting in the unpredictable currents of a roaring river. For the first year and a half after graduating college, I smashed boulders with a sledgehammer, broke drywall with my fists, tore down old, brittle wood from dilapidated houses, and then fixed and painted them anew.

And then one day my life changed and a career began. It was the day my beloved father got me a part-time job at NBC Sports. That day is indelibly etched in my being.

It was a beautiful Sunday afternoon in early September. Clear blue skies, thin air, a slight breeze ruffling through the colorful leaves of red maple, yellow oak and white elm. A quintessential fall day in New York City. A day that made you feel you were living in a Mark Twain fairy tale, one painted by Norman Rockwell. A day that anything imaginable seemed possible.

And indeed it was.

I saw none of that, except on my twenty-minute drive along the scenic Palisades Interstate Parkway into the city of bright lights. Instead of sunshine and warmth, I spent this day inside the cool, windowless studios of 30 Rockefeller Plaza, the home of NBC Sports, staring at a myriad of television monitors that showcased every NFL game that was airing live across the nation. It was the first day my dream, and my future legacy, blossomed into being.

That day my job was as a "logger." I'd be assigned one NFL football game to watch, and detail each play of that game with pen on paper. I would chronicle how many yards were gained, whether it was a pass, a run or a trick play, and record the "timecode" (the exact time of day) the play occurred. I'd highlight each big play in yellow. Big plays were touchdowns, turnovers, sacks and all things crucial that told the story of the game. Then an associate producer would use my notes to edit a highlight package to be used during the halftime and postgame shows. The highlight packages were constantly updated and changed, depending on the ebb and flow of the game.

"What is your favorite team?" was the question my new boss, Cary Glotzer, asked me with a smile on that first day.

"The New York Jets," I replied. His smile widened.

"Mine too!"

"Really?"

"Yes! So I have an assignment that is going to make you very happy today."

"What is that?"

"Your assignment is to watch the Jets game and write down a written log of every play of the game."

"For real?"

"Yes, for real. I know your dad very well and I have a good feeling about you. Plus you smile a lot."

"So do you!"

Glotzer's smile widened even more as he patted me on the back and left. Pinch me, I thought. This felt like a dream. A smiling, inspiring boss, a positive work atmosphere, and I was getting paid to watch my beloved New York Jets play football.

Each week when the game I was tasked to log was over, and all the highlight packages had been edited, I'd walk up two floors to the live studio set and become a "gopher." In television lingo that means "go for this" and "go get that" for either the studio hosts or any executive who was present.

"Can you get me a cup of coffee?" were the first words Bob Costas, the lead host of the show *NFL Live*, said to me.

"Sure thing," I responded. "How would you like that, Mr. Costas?"

"Black with one packet of Sweet'n Low."

"Coming right up."

The next week, Costas asked the same favor of me.

"Black with one Sweet'n Low, Mr. Costas?" I asked. He looked at me with affirmation and an inquisitive smile.

"How did you know that, young man?" he asked.

"That's the way you asked me to make it last week, and it's my job to remember."

My kinship with Costas began in that moment. He recognized the passion, positivity and potential that I exuded, appreciated my youthful zest. Me? I was just honored to be assisting this smart, articulate, Emmy Award–winning television personality that had so much passion for the job he loved, too.

When the football season was over, Glotzer asked if I wanted to remain at NBC as a logger for the rest of the year. It was basketball and hockey season now, and soon it would be opening day for Major League Baseball. After getting a taste of what I loved, the decision to stay was easy.

Less than a year later, I also became a part-time production assistant for the NBC Sports on-air promotion department. My boss was John Schipp, and we bonded instantly. Schipp became my mentor, I his respectful and grateful protégé. He was extremely creative, but at the same time deeply frustrated by the constraints that were placed upon him. Just a few months later, I was made a permanent, salaried employee of the department, with paid benefits. It was a tiny group, just four of us at first, not including the editors and engineers in the edit rooms where we would produce promotional spots for our upcoming sports events.

Schipp resigned his post just two years later, frustrated by the corporate world. There were two writer/producers in the department at that time, both of whom were above me in the pecking order, and they both interviewed for the position — as did I, a mere production associate. Against all odds I got the job, and at age twenty-six became the youngest person ever to hold the title of "manager, on-air promotions" for a major broadcast network. My peers at ABC, CBS and Fox Sports were all in their late forties or fifties.

I attribute my meteoric rise to one simple fact, a lesson I now preach to all who are still searching for what they want to become in life: I was passionate about the work. Find your passion, whatever it is that brings you joy in life, then get an entry-level job in that profession and bust your butt. If you truly love that field and are willing to work long, hard hours, you will become incredibly successful, incredibly fast. Why? Because you love what you are doing.

I made a name for myself in a very short time. In addition to managing on-air promotions for NBC Sports, I produced campaigns for the NFL, MLB, the NBA, the PGA Tour, Wimbledon and the Barcelona Olympics. And it all happened because I truly loved what I was doing.

That simple. That is truly the key to happiness and success.

2

LEAVING NBC

Over time I too became frustrated with the hierarchy at NBC Sports. There was a new president in Dick Ebersol, and he'd brought a few of his favorite cronies with him. Most of the executives remaining from the previous regime soon became cronies, too. (False ones, though.)

There's hardly a bad thing I can say about Dick. He was a great visionary and incredibly creative. Ebersol changed the world of late-night television when he helped launch *Saturday Night Live*, and now he was tasked with making NBC Sports relevant again. And he did.

On both a professional and personal level, Ebersol showed tremendous respect for me, so I respected him very much in return.

The cronies, however, I viewed as frauds.

On Ebersol's first day in the corporate offices of NBC Sports, he arrived wearing a navy blue suit, red-striped tie and blue suspenders. And he was puffing on a mighty large cigar. Within a few days the associates closest to him were doing the same. Cigar smoke became ubiquitous in the entire executive wing of NBC Sports.

Ebersol's cronies were also very conservative. Every time I tried to be innovative with a promotional campaign, they reeled me in. I wanted to be creative, add new flavors and colors to the tapestry of mainstream sports promotion, and throw in a little hot sauce. That is not what they wanted. They wanted vanilla.

When NBC Sports first landed the NBA for the 1990–91 season, I created a commercial spot with the tag, "The NBA on NBC: Come Fly with Us." This spot highlighted the greatest stars of the day doing incredible feats in a fashion that was quick-cutting and fitting, in an MTV style (when MTV was still cutting-edge and relevant). The iconic voice of James Earl Jones was what I envisioned for the narration. We even put thunderous sound effects on every dunk. I thought the spot itself was a slam dunk, too. The powers that be did not.

They dismissed my idea and instead directed me to produce a piece that was cut to the theme song from the famous play *Annie*, and I was told to use all slow-motion shots. Bad idea, I thought. Slow motion was the antithesis of the fast and frenetic pace of an NBA game. Worse, I was then told:

"On the line 'the sun will come out tomorrow,' use a shot of Charles Barkley."

"Okay."

"Do you know why?"

"No."

"Because he plays for the Phoenix Suns. Get it?"

Yes, I get it. But the simplistic logic sickened my stomach.

Their concept for the initial promotional campaign did not feel right. The NBA was electrifying and exciting. This spot they wanted captured none of that. I was also told to use only two stars of color at a time. A white player had to be featured every third shot. After Larry Bird, John Paxson and Chris Mullin, there were very few choices.

In their minds, they weren't being racist. They wanted the commercial to appeal to mainstream America. I knew better. Racist they were. And mainstream American viewers were already way ahead of the perceptions the older executives and cronies had. They were thrilled by the electrifying heroics of stars like Michael Jordan, Magic Johnson and Charles Barkley, regardless of color. They were enamored with the fast-paced action of the NBA.

A year later, I produced a spot for the women's final at Wimbledon. It ended with a shot of Martina Navratilova raising the coveted trophy. Then I was called up to the executive floor to discuss the promo.

"Why did you end the spot with a shot of Martina Navratilova?" I was asked after the spot was screened before going on air.

"She's been in the finals nine years in a row, and won the tournament a record six straight," I replied. "And she's also the defending champion. Why would we *not* end the spot with a shot of Martina Navratilova holding the trophy high above her head?"

One executive nodded. He seemed convinced by my rationale.

"I don't care," the other responded. "Whenever I see her I see a dyke."

The silent, nodding crony kept nodding, then turned his nodding head to his superior.

"I agree," he said. "I thought the very same thing."

Read into that what you wish. (It's blatantly obvious.) My disenchantment grew.

In August of 1992, I received a phone call from John Filippelli, also known as "Flip," the executive vice president of production for the WWF. Two years earlier, Flip had left NBC Sports and become the most powerful man in the WWF besides Vince McMahon. He was McMahon's right-hand guy. During his tenure at NBC, Flip was one of the most amazing and highly regarded producers who ever worked there. His passion was baseball. He was legendary. Although I never worked with Flip at NBC, we would often chat in the halls and offices at 30 Rock. He acknowledged he was fond of the flair and creativity in the promos I created, especially when it came to the NFL and MLB.

"David," Flip said, "we are looking for a new creative director for our on-air promotions department at the WWF. Would you be interested?"

"I'm flattered," I hesitantly replied. "Thanks, but I'm not sure."

"It's a fun environment here," Flip said. "And I'll pay you nearly twice what you are earning at NBC. You know you are grossly underpaid there."

"Let me think about it."

"If you can, I'd like you to come to Stamford sometime next week and visit us. I will get you a meeting with Vince McMahon, too. He is a fan of your work."

And so I went.

The very next week, I arrived at Titan Towers in Stamford, Connecticut, after a one-hour train ride from New York City's Grand Central Station, sporting a navy blue blazer, pressed white shirt and a blue silk tie. Vince was wearing gaudy, colorful sweatpants of white, black and red, and a matching sweatshirt. He looked like a "meathead," and he was playing with a remote toy car in his office when I walked in. He was having fun. And when he first saw me he smiled broadly, shook my hand, and politely asked me to have a seat at his table. Right away I sensed he had a certain power and charm I had never felt before. Charisma oozed from every one of his pores.

He is the devil incarnate, I first thought, but he's so damn charming and I want to believe him. Maybe what everyone else says about him is wrong.

"David," Vince said, "thank you for coming. What we do here is have fun." Then he proceeded with his convincing sales pitch, delivered with delight, describing what my job would entail. Most appealing about his pitch was that the job would unburden me from the corporate constraints I was bound to at NBC Sports. It would allow me to unleash the creativity within, something I tried to do and was denied. Something I deeply craved.

"Vince, you make this job sound so appealing, *I* want it!" Flip joked when Vince was finished.

"I would want it, too," Vince replied.

I was intrigued. And impressed. Now it was no longer a distant dream. Joining the WWF had suddenly become a very serious option.

I pondered this decision for nearly six weeks. The WWF gave me great latitude. Finally, Flip called.

"David, it's been weeks," he reminded me. "What is your delay?"

"I just want to meet with Dick Ebersol."

"We can't wait much longer," Flip said. "Please tell me yes or no by the end of this week, because if it's no I need to find someone else."

"I understand, and thanks for your patience. I will schedule a meeting with Ken Schanzer tomorrow and make my decision by the end of the week, Flip. I promise."

Ebersol had just returned to the States from the Barcelona Olympics two weeks earlier and was not in the office. He was enjoying a much-needed reprieve at his home in Litchfield, Connecticut. Schanzer, the executive vice president of NBC Sports, Ebersol's right-hand man and number-one crony, had full control of the reins during this time.

The next morning I went to Schanzer's office and told him I had a tempting offer from the WWF and wanted a counter.

"I'd rather stay here," I told Schanzer, "but they are offering a lot of money. Can you meet me halfway?"

Schanzer knew how underpaid I was at NBC because of my youth. My peers at the other networks were making at least three times more than me. It was something NBC blatantly took advantage of.

"Let's meet again tomorrow at 10 a.m.," Schanzer replied. "I want to think about this overnight."

The next day came, and a life-changing decision loomed. Hopefully Schanzer would offer me a slight raise so that I could stay. For what seemed like an hour, Schanzer kept me waiting before inviting me into his office. He spoke first.

"David, you are underpaid," he said, sitting in a leather chair, feet up on his dark wooden desk, his hand tapping a lead pencil. "And you deserve a raise."

"Thank you."

"However, I couldn't sleep last night," Schanzer continued. "I thought the 'love of the Peacock' is the reason you should stay, not money. So although you deserve a raise, I will not give you one at this time."

I was stunned. Shock then turned to silent fury. I knew Schanzer thought I was bluffing, believing I would never leave NBC for the WWF. My answer was immediate.

"Then as of today I give you my two-week notice."

"Are you serious?" he asked as I stood up.

"Quite serious," I replied, then walked out the door.

The first thing I did was call Flip and tell him I was joining the WWF. He was overjoyed. Tears filled my eyes when the magnitude of the moment sunk in. As I told my co-workers and voice-over announcers the news, they teared up as well.

"This can't be true," said Jim Fagan, our lead voice-over artist, emotion garbling his manly voice on the phone. "They can't do this to you, David. That's wrong."

"They just did," I replied.

"Damn them."

"Would you be willing to do voice-over work for me at the WWF?" I asked.

"Yes. In a heartbeat, because it's for you."

"Then you will be the new voice of the WWF on the very first spot I produce."

True to my word, I gave NBC my best those final two weeks. Two days before my departure, Ebersol returned and immediately summoned me to his office. I obliged. I respected this legendary leader.

"David, please have a seat on the couch," Ebersol said when I entered his expansive corner office. Then he rose from his desk and sat down beside me on the couch. He wasn't just a boss in that moment. This move was his way of telling me he was also a father-like figure, a friend.

"Did Schanzer really say he wouldn't give you a raise?"

"Yes he did."

"That is ridiculous. I had no idea this was going on or I would have made sure we didn't lose you. I want you to stay, and I will match that offer you have from Vince to keep you here."

"Dick, I'm a man of my word. Even though I wanted to stay, I will not renege on my decision. They showed great patience and it's not fair to them for me to do that now."

A moment of silence. Ebersol looked down, gathered his thoughts, then offered a revelation.

"Vince is a dear friend of mine," he said with slight remorse. "And I never knew Vince would do this to me. This hurts on a visceral level. Are you sure I can't convince you to stay?"

I told him again that I couldn't go back on my word, and another silent moment passed.

"David, I wish you luck," Ebersol finally said, rising to shake my hand. "Just don't get lost in that world of sports entertainment. You will always have a home here if you choose to come back."

"Thank you, Dick. That means more than you know. And one day I just might."

Minutes later, I was told, Ebersol walked into a boardroom and, in front of a dozen or so chairmen, he belittled and berated Schanzer for nearly ten minutes for having the audacity to let me leave.

Hearing that did not bring me pleasure. It brought something far greater.

It brought validation.

3

JOINING THE WWF

My first experience as an employee for the WWF was surreal to say the least. I was flown into Regina, Canada, in the evening and, because I forgot my passport, was detained in customs for nearly two hours. When I arrived at the hotel around midnight, I beheld the amazing sight of The Undertaker checking in at Red Roof, where all the talent and most of the employees were staying.

The next day I was driven to the venue by George Germanakos, a production assistant at the time. The first characters I saw backstage were Doink the Clown, Duke "The Dumpster" Droese, and in an adjacent room I saw Kamala, "The Ugandan Giant," in full face paint and reading *The New York Times* intently. He never spoke on TV. Being naïve about this strange new world, I really believed he was incapable of speech. Then he saw me.

"Are you the new guy?" Kamala asked, peering over his newspaper. I was stunned.

"Yes. My name is David."

He rose, this giant of a man, and shook my hand. He was two feet taller than I, and his hand was twice the size of mine. When we shook, it was like a catcher's mitt grabbing a baseball. Yet he greeted me gently and with great warmth before resuming his seat.

"David, do you have any money invested in stocks?"

"Not currently."

"Then you should start. Let me give you some advice. Here are some secrets." And so Kamala, the giant from the forests of Africa who most thought was incapable of speech, spent fifteen minutes articulating what to invest in and what to avoid.

I was dumbfounded. I had come from the world of "real" sports, having worked with superstars such as Michael Jordan, Don Mattingly, Bo Jackson, Magic Johnson and Jack Nicklaus, to name a few. Now I was amid a world of fantasy and a carnival of characters, not knowing what was real and what was mere illusion.

As I continued my strange stroll through the inner bowels of the arena, another renowned star approached me.

"So, you're the new guy," said Pat Patterson, a writer, producer, agent and part of the creative team at the time. Patterson was also famous for being the first-ever Intercontinental Champion in WWF history.

"You look like a gimmick!" Patterson added with a laugh.

In a way I did. I was wearing a navy blue sports jacket, dark tan slacks, blue suspenders and a black fedora, adorning my head, while everyone else was dressed in casual business attire or wearing a costume.

"I've got a question for you," Patterson continued. "If you woke up in a hotel room with a really bad hangover, no memory of what happened, and a condom sticking out of your ass, would you tell anyone?"

"Oh god no!" I responded.

"Good!" he shouted with glee while patting my shoulder. "Then what are you doing tonight after the show?"

He was joking of course. Pat Patterson would soon become one of my most beloved friends, a man I truly admired. But I didn't know him just yet, so I was bewildered.

Then a few minutes later I ran into Owen Hart.

"Hi," he said in a soft, submissive voice.

"Hi."

"I'm Owen."

"I'm David."

I knew who he was, but he was acting strange. Then he proceeded to purposely stalk me for almost two straight hours. Wherever I walked, wherever I went, he would appear.

"Hi, I'm Owen," he would say each and every time I saw him. He appeared as if he was a super-fan or had some kind of crush on me. I had no idea at the time he was merely acting. Then out of nowhere his best friend, "The British Bulldog," strapped a master lock on my belt loop and locked it to my trousers, laughing the whole time, and kept the key until the show was over.

Don't get me wrong. These wrestlers and producers weren't bullying me or being mean. These were just "ribs," as they say in the world of professional wrestling. It was their way of welcoming me, letting me know I was appreciated and now a part of the fraternity. Coming from the no-nonsense world of NBC Sports, however, it just felt so different, so unreal.

An hour later, Flip walked me to the television production truck that was parked underneath the arena.

"This is Kevin Dunn," Flip told me as Dunn was walking up the steel steps that led into the truck to produce episodes of *WWF Superstars*. Dunn was the number two person in production, behind only Filippelli. He didn't smile, and I sensed an attitude of disdain. From all the stories I had heard, by reputation Dunn carried a dark, sinister person within.

"I've heard good things about you," I told Dunn, acting as if I'd never heard the rumors.

"Don't believe any of it," he replied, cold-faced and stoic. And by the look on his face, I knew he was dead serious, not yet ready to welcome this newcomer, this outsider from NBC Sports, into his world.

What I'd heard about Kevin Dunn was that he was extremely talented, yet ruthless and vengeful. Rumors were he greatly disliked his boss, Flip, and believed he should have been appointed executive producer of the WWF years earlier. He did not like being number two, especially to an "outsider" like Flip, even though Filippelli was an award-winning baseball producer who came from NBC Sports. (In time, the rumors about Dunn would prove true.)

Finally, just before the show, Vince invited me into his office. It was a tiny venue, and the barren office was just slightly larger than a walk-in closet. We were talking one-on-one now for the first time since he became my boss.

"David, what we do here is all about emotion," Vince said with a proud, genuine smile. "We have fun with what we do. So just have fun and don't look at it as a job."

Vince was speaking about the matches, the storylines that brought the adversaries into the ring to battle. But his words resonated with me on a deeper, visceral level.

I knew what I had to do, and that was make sure every one of my promotional productions — whether it be a commercial spot, a cold open for a pay-per-view, or an ad campaign for the world to see — would be filled with emotion. I wanted the audience, the fans, to feel something on an intuitive level.

Vince inspired me with those words. In that moment, he gave me the freedom to rise and soar, something I was never fully given at NBC Sports. He gave me the wings I needed to fly.

4

THE FIRST *RAW* OPENING

Three weeks in.

That's when the phone call came.

"Sahadi," Kevin Dunn said, calling from his office in Stamford, Connecticut, while I was in a graphics studio in New York City.

"Flip is gone. So is John Blank, and . . ."

Dunn proceeded to go down a list of fifteen to twenty NBC employees who joined the WWF years earlier for the World Bodybuilding Federation, an ambitious dream that became a nightmare one year later. Now they had all been fired in a single day. It was a bloodletting. It was unsettling. In my mind, trusting intuition over facts, it felt like a coup.

"If I had my way," Dunn continued, "your NBC ass would be gone, too. But Vince likes you and wants to give you a chance. So this opening for *Monday Night Raw* that you are working on better be good, or you're fucking gone, too."

And then he hung up. Instantly. Before I could fully comprehend. Before I could even utter a single reply. That was the Kevin Dunn I'd been warned about. This was the first time I saw the dark, dictatorial side of Dunn, and it wouldn't be the last.

Only three weeks in.

I was stunned. It felt like the final scene from *The Godfather* when Al Pacino, playing the role of Michael Corleone, finally assumed ultimate power and had all of his enemies killed. I knew I'd be next if I didn't deliver a slick, cutting-edge opening for a new show that would be debuting in January of 1993. And I also knew Kevin Dunn's loyal regime wanted me to fail, too. After all, I was an outsider, the lone former NBC employee still working there.

"Could I get my old job back at NBC?" was one of the first thoughts that popped in my head.

"If I get fired and can't get my old job back, what will I do next?" was another.

A few minutes later I found the key to my destiny. It was simple. It came from within. This opening would be great, the best one the WWF had ever had. I was determined to make it so. Actually, I had no choice.

For the next two weeks I split my time between the graphics suite in New York City and the production studios in Stamford. I felt the pressure piled on me, but my trio of production staff in Stamford had faith, and it was their faith that inspired me.

"I'm excited to see what you do," said Larry Rochman, my top producer in the on-air promotions department.

"It'll be different," I replied. "Very different, unlike anything they've seen before. That's all I can guarantee."

The day of judgment came one Sunday in December. I was sitting in my office in Stamford on a cold and cloudy afternoon when Dunn called from the studios below.

"We are ready to view the show open. Bring it down to the control room and put it on VTR 1."

I carried the tape downstairs to master control and gave it to the lead technician to load on the playback machine. Then I walked into the edit room.

The mood in the room was somber and unsettling. Present were Vince McMahon, Kevin Dunn, Bruce Prichard, Pat Patterson, Kevin Quinn, the lead editor, the lead audio engineer, Kevin Neal, George Germanakos, and a few others.

"Is it loaded?" Dunn asked.

"Yes it is."

"Play it," Dunn told the editor.

And the opening video was first seen by everyone that mattered, all those who would decide my fate.

The opening contained multiple layers of video footage that were overlaid and intercut with graphics and animation in blue, red and black-and-white tones. Featured were WWF superstars Razor Ramon, Bret "The Hitman" Hart and The Undertaker, to name a few. The music was powerful, featuring an electric guitar and a beat dominated by a driving percussion and drums, and it ended with the sound of a police siren echoing over the red *Raw* logo.

The screening was over quickly, since the spot was only twenty-three seconds long, and the response was . . . silence. Not a single person spoke or moved. Vince lowered his head for thirty seconds, deep in thought, then turned and walked to the coffee machine ten feet behind him. He poured a cup of black coffee into a white Styrofoam cup, took a pink packet of Sweet'n Low and shook it seven or eight times before emptying it into his cup. By this point the silence was deafening. Then he added more sweetener, took a sip, and walked back to his previous spot before finally saying something.

"Play it again."

So they watched it again, and when it finished, this time McMahon looked up and stared silently at the ceiling for nearly a minute. His expression was solemn, shadowed by uncertainty. I sensed he didn't "feel it." The room remained dark and silent. Again no one spoke or moved. Except for Vince.

"Well, what do you all think?" Vince finally asked the room.

"I like it!" Bruce Prichard quickly said with exuberance. "It's different."

"And so is the music," another chimed in.

"I really like the multiple layers of video," said a third.

"Someone obviously likes Razor Ramon," was Dunn's lone comment.

"The police siren gives it an edge and a sense of danger and taboo," added another.

"Then let's go with it," Vince decided.

The time it took for someone to speak after this short spot was shown, not once but twice, was nearly ten minutes, but to me it felt like hours.

All the while I assumed they were not happy and I was done, but I was wrong. I had delivered. I'd dodged my first bullet — my heart found its beat again, and my spirit first sighed then smiled.

To be honest, looking back now the video is not as great as I once thought. But it was different and far ahead of anything they had produced before.

Truth be told, the reason we created *Monday Night Raw* was because the company was hemorrhaging money. We called it *Raw* because the show and the set were stripped down, free of all the high costs of top-end production. *Raw* sounded edgy — and eventually, during the Attitude Era, it was (more on this in chapter 8) — but the show was created out of necessity, an attempt to save money and keep the company afloat. That simple. That raw.

Through my entire eleven-year tenure, I was tasked with producing all the openings for *Monday Night Raw*. The second opening was the memorable "Raw on the Roof" shoot that was filmed on September 7, 1995. It was considered by one wrestling writer as "the WWF's most ambitious production to date."

The shoot took place atop the WWF headquarters in Stamford. The concept called for a rooftop party with superstars battling it out high above the street. A crane was enlisted to move ring equipment from the ground level, and a helicopter was flown in to capture aerial footage. A shot of the helicopter taken from the ground as it lowered itself from the sky, a full moon glowing behind it, was used in the open's iconic first shot. Hundreds of WWF fans from the surrounding neighborhood joined in as extras. Shawn Michaels was seen from above and below dancing high in the shadows of the huge WWF logo before eventually doing an elbow drop into the ring, twenty feet below. There were also cheerleaders, Michael Hayes singing with a band, police officers frantically trying to close the party down, and a forty-foot blow-up model of The Undertaker.

The result?

"One of the most famous scenes ever in WWE history," in the opinion of another wrestling reporter.

A few days later, after the opening was edited, Vince McMahon had a few suggestions for additional "pickup" scenes.

"Let's do a few more scenes to make it comedic," McMahon said. "Like have a shot of the cops trying to open the doors and they can't because there is peanut butter on the handles. And let's have some of the policemen running up the stairs like the Keystone Cops and slip and fall on banana peels."

What a horrible idea, I thought. It was amateurish humor. This opening had an edge and an air of defiance. Silly comedy would diminish that. Thankfully, he was talked out of it.

My favorite *Raw* opening to this day remains the "Raw Is War" shoot we produced in 1997. The concept was fire, fury, madness and mayhem.

The shoot took place in an abandoned shipping warehouse on the docks of Brooklyn, New York, on a cold December night. A ring was set up on a frigid concrete floor above the choppy waters of New York Harbor. Scenes of war were projected on the background walls while WWF superstars fought in a ring that was literally set on fire. Stone Cold Steve Austin walked through huge fireballs of explosions without even a flinch as he calmly made his way to the ring. The soundtrack started with loud sirens warning of an imminent missile attack over an exterior shot of an abandoned building, taken using a fifty-foot crane. The spot really had an apocalyptic feel.

A New York City fire marshal was present for the shoot, making sure we were abiding by the laws regarding pyrotechnics and explosions of gasoline mixed with propane. He had one objection.

"I will not allow you to set the ropes on fire."

"Why not?" I politely asked.

"Because it could be a fire hazard."

"How so? This is an abandoned warehouse and there is nothing but steel beams and concrete rubble. Nothing here could catch fire."

"I still won't allow it."

Then my producer, Dave "Derk" Anderko, stepped in.

"Why can't we set the ropes on fire?"

"Because it's a fire hazard," the fire marshal repeated.

Derk was prepared for this moment. He proceeded to peel \$100 bills from a wad in his pocket until the count reached five. The marshal took notice.

"Would you be willing to take a coffee break soon?" Derk asked pointedly as he started to hand over the money.

"Sure," the marshal said. "When would you like me to go?"

"How about now?"

"Okay," he replied as Derk handed him the $500. "When would you like me to come back?"

"In an hour. Maybe two."

"Thank you. I could use a hot cup of coffee now to warm me up," he said as he turned and left the premises.

Time to burn! We set the ring ropes on fire as over a dozen WWF superstars battled within the flaming ring. An hour later, when the fire marshal returned, the red ropes were charred black and gray, obviously having been set aflame. He took notice and smiled, yet remained silent. He had his $500 in cash in his pocket. He was very happy.

At one point Vince McMahon showed up in a limousine. He knew it was cold and the abandoned warehouse had no heat. He looked around, noticed a dozen empty pizza boxes, a few cases of bottled water, and nothing else.

"Where's the catering?" he angrily asked.

"It's late," I replied. "It should be here soon."

"You bring these guys out here to a cold dump in the middle of nowhere and there is no hot food to eat? That's not only disgraceful, it's disrespectful!"

He turned to the boys and proceeded to thank each and every one, assuring them that hot food was on its way.

I knew what McMahon was doing. He wasn't really mad at me personally. He knew we did nothing wrong. He merely wanted the boys, dressed in their wrestling gear on a cold December night, to know he was looking out for them. It was his way of expressing that he had their backs. That's what great leaders do, so I took no offense.

The final production was well received by all and even garnered my second Promax Gold Medallion Award, which honors creative excellence in television production.

Producing those opens for *Monday Night Raw* brought me so much pleasure. The creativity nourished my soul, and breaking new ground with very few limits and constraints fueled me. I am blessed and honored to have produced each one during my tenure there.

And I was also heartened because I knew these opens would soon lead to the creation of the greatest boom in professional wrestling history, one that would become known as the Attitude Era.

5

MY FIRST COMMERCIALS

The first commercial spots I produced and directed were humorous. Yes, I would present the stars as real athletes shortly, but I thought some clever comedy would be a great transition from the cartoon land of pro wrestling to the real world.

One of my favorite spots was for the initial "King of the Ring" pay-per-view event featuring, of course, Jerry "The King" Lawler. The event would take place in November, so the theme was a Thanksgiving feast featuring Lawler as the ultimate heel.

The spot opens with a shot of Lawler enjoying a gluttonous Thanksgiving feast. Then two skinny, starved adolescents with outstretched plates ask a question:

"Please, King, may we have some more?"

Lawler hands a turkey leg to his dog sitting beside him. "Get lost, brats!" he says.

At that moment he chokes on a piece of food and apparently dies. Next we see him standing alone in a white wrestling ring surrounded by endless white clouds and smoke.

"Ah, heaven!" he exclaims. "The great ring in the sky. I truly am The King."

But then all the other kings show up.

First he gets whacked in the back by a guitar and falls to the canvas. It's quickly revealed to have been swung by Elvis Presley.

"Not so fast, Lawler," Elvis proclaims.

"We'll see who's king around here," King Tut adds, as Don King nods his head and smiles.

"He's no king! He's no king!" chant other iconic kings of the past, accompanied by a dog wearing a king's crown.

Eventually King Kong gives him a body slam, and Elvis pushes his face into the ring's bottom turnbuckle with his boot.

"Where am I?" Lawler screams in anguish. Then we cut to a shot of the devil, played by Vince McMahon himself, face painted red, who looks into the camera and delivers a sinister laugh.

Bret Hart was also featured in an iconic spot. It was a takeoff on the Mean Joe Greene Coca-Cola commercial that debuted a year earlier during the Super Bowl.

In this spot, we see Hart walking backstage on the way to the ring. A father and son just happen to notice this.

"That's Bret 'The Hitman' Hart!" the young boy exuberantly tells his father.

"Be quiet, son," the father gently says. "He's getting ready for the big match."

The young boy cannot contain his excitement. "Bret!" he yells, his voice echoing through the tunnel leading to the arena.

Hart stops upon hearing the boy's scream. As the camera quickly zooms in, Hart slowly turns around, and then with great deliberation and purpose walks back to the boy in a way that seems menacing. The father and son are silent and uneasy. After one more moment of tension, Bret smiles, takes the pink shades off his face and puts them on the boy's eyes. The kid is overjoyed.

"Go get him, Champ!" he tells Hart, who smiles and heads to the ring.

In early 1994, I produced a series of three spots called "Church Confessionals." The first one featured a young man in a confessional booth apologizing for his sins. Every time he would tell the priest a sin he committed, such as cheating on his wife, the priest would seemingly applaud his actions with words of approval. The young man gets confused. How could his deplorable actions be justified?

"Father," he eventually says. "Father, can you hear me?"

Then we cut to the priest's point of view. He has headphones covering both ears as he watches the WWF on a small television. The priest, an obvious WWF fan, was actually reacting to the wrestling moves he was watching, oblivious to what the young man had said.

The tagline was "The WWF: Put Your Faith in Us."

The payoff, the final spot in the trilogy, featured Razor Ramon.

"Yo, Father," Razor says in a tight shot of his face, toothpick in mouth. "Last night, I hurt someone real bad."

"Elaborate, my son," the priest replies. "What provoked this act?"

"I wanted his belt, man."

"My son, haven't we always been told not to covet thy neighbor's goods?"

"Yes, man, but he took the first swipe."

"Haven't we always been told to turn the other cheek?"

"Yes Father. But when he took that swipe, he broke my toothpick. So I picked him up high and then slammed him to the ground."

"You slammed a man to the ground because he broke your toothpick? Who do you think you are — Razor Ramon?"

We cut to a shot of the toothpick dropping from Razor's mouth.

"Hey Father, how did you know?" The priest turns to face him for the first time and is astonished. We then cut to the tag page, and when we go back to the priest he's eagerly asking Razor Ramon for autographed photos.

"And this one's for Father John," the priest says. "Oh, and this one's for Sister Elizabeth!"

Later in 1994, Major League Baseball players went on strike. The owners and the players union could not come to terms, so the World Series was canceled. Immediately I told Vince an idea I had to capitalize on this. He smiled, and within a day McMahon called NBC and purchased a thirty-second spot to air the following weekend on NBC Sports while the news was still fresh. Ebersol was Vince's friend, and I believe that played a part in making this happen so quickly.

I had three days to produce, shoot, write and edit this piece before sending it to NBC for approval. The concept featured a young boy alone at a local baseball field who is saddened that the baseball season is over. As he walks around the park with a baseball bat in his hands, we hear iconic calls from legendary baseball broadcasters during the game's most memorable moments.

"Groundball to first base . . . through his legs!"

"The Giants win the pennant! The Giants win the pennant!"

"He's done it again! Three home runs in one game."

"What a classic!"

The boy smiles — until a more somber announcer's call takes over.

"Ladies and gentlemen, for the first time in modern history there will be no World Series this year."

The boy becomes saddened and drops his glove, the baseball rolling out onto the red clay of the pitcher's mound.

"In an era where promises are often broken . . ." begins the soft, heartwarming voice of a legendary announcer, Peter Thomas.

Then we see the Macho Man, Randy Savage, approach the boy.

"Hey kid," Savage says. "Let's hit a few."

The boy's eyes light up as he races to the batter's box.

"One federation and its superstars still believe in making dreams come true," the announcer continues.

The Macho Man goes to the pitcher's mound, and as the boy swings, a thunderous sound is heard. We cut to the tag page as the WWF announcer proudly declares, "The World Wrestling Federation: Our season never ends."

The spot aired on NBC the entire weekend. The executives of both companies were proud. Although I had won an Emmy Award at NBC Sports, this was the second award I won working for the WWF. It was a Silver Telly Award. The previous trophy was a Promax Gold Medallion Award for the "Unbelievable" campaign we'd filmed a few months earlier.

Silver and gold. Most would be proud. Me? Not satisfied. Not yet anyway. I was just warming up. My best creative ideas, and a multitude of award-winning spots, were yet to come.

6

WRESTLEMANIA CELEBRITIES

Whenever the WWF would present WrestleMania, its biggest pay-per-view of the year, there would always be a plethora of celebrities who were paid to be present and take part in the event. Muhammad Ali, Liberace, the Rockettes and Cyndi Lauper were just a few that would be part of WrestleMania I.

Often these celebrities would be featured in promotional spots leading up to the event in an attempt to attract a mainstream audience, people who weren't enslaved in the wrestling bubble. One of my favorites was WrestleMania XI in 1995. The A-list included Pamela Anderson, Jenny McCarthy, Nicholas Turturro, Jonathan Taylor Thomas and Hall of Fame linebacker Lawrence Taylor, who was booked in a match against Bam Bam Bigelow.

That year, I was tasked with shooting promotional spots with Anderson, Turturro and Taylor. Three months before, at the Royal Rumble, Anderson was there to shoot five promos with Shawn Michaels, which we would air over the final five weeks leading up to WrestleMania. It was announced that Anderson would accompany the winner of the Royal Rumble down the aisle at WrestleMania, and it was ordained that Michaels would win the event that night.

The day of the Rumble, Anderson arrived four hours late. She was dating Tommy Lee at the time, and when she arrived it seemed she was under the influence of something. What that was I didn't know or care; she had shown up, and that's all that mattered to me. We gave her two hours in hair and makeup and then she was ready for the shoot.

In less than two hours we had four spots in the can, just one more to shoot. As we started shooting the fifth one, the opening video of WrestleMania began playing and Shawn Michaels asked a question.

"David, can we take a quick break so that I can watch the opening to the show?"

"Of course," I replied.

In the room where we were shooting these vignettes, there was also a "hard camera" and if you looked into this camera you could see the "return" of what was airing live to the world. Why it was there I was not sure. Perhaps just in case they needed an emergency live backstage interview later in the show.

Shawn, Pamela and I looked into the camera. We saw the opening pyro exploding in grand fashion, as well as shots of the frenzied fans. A few seconds in, suddenly a three-shot of Pamela, Shawn and myself staring into the camera like three deer in the headlights appeared on live television. Quickly the director cut away to show more crowd shots. We were shocked and confused.

"Was that a shot of us just now?" Shawn asked with concern.

"I think so," I nervously replied.

"Did that air live?'

"I'm pretty sure it did."

Damn, we were screwed. Someone in the television production truck — either the director or technical director, who "punches" the camera shots on the switcher — took a shot of us by accident, and it was a horrible mistake. We had just given away the finish of the Royal Rumble, and everyone who was watching probably knew that.

Immediately someone came to the rescue. It was the legendary play-by-play announcer Jim Ross, who was calling the show.

"Well you just saw a shot of Shawn Michaels schmoozing Pamela Anderson backstage. He's a cocky bastard and he obviously thinks he's going to win the Rumble tonight."

What a cover. Thank you, Jim Ross!

Working with Nicholas Turturro was fun. Turturro was one of the stars of the hit TV show *NYPD Blue* at the time.

Two months before WrestleMania, we shot five promos with Turturro to air in the weeks before the event. These commercial spots were filmed on a studio set that resembled *NYPD Blue*. We even used the show's shaky-camera style. The pieces felt legit.

Of the five spots, my favorite was the one where Turturro grills Paul Bearer, with rival manager Mr. Fuji present. Bearer had been accused of an egregious crime. The ongoing WWF storyline was that Yokozuna, the former world champion who Fuji managed, had gone missing for nearly six months.

"We got a problem here, Mr. Paul Bearer," Turturro says. "This man has been missing since November. We suspect foul play here and you're our number one suspect."

Turturro then drops a manila envelope full of pictures of Yokozuna.

"But why me, Detective Turturro?" Bearer asks off-screen as we cut to a shot of Fuji smiling.

"We got eyewitnesses that saw you at the crime scene," Turturro continues. "And we have your fingerprints all over the coffin."

"But I haven't done anything wrong," replies Bearer as the camera pans over, showing him in a blond wig and a dress.

"Then why have you been in hiding?"

"Hiding? I haven't been hiding."

"Then how do you explain the dress?"

"Dress? What dress?"

Suddenly we hear the gong of The Undertaker.

"Yes! He's here!" Bearer exclaims just before the lights are suddenly turned off, sending the room into total blackness.

"What the hell is this?" Turturro asks.

One second later the lights are back on, and now it is Mr. Fuji wearing the dress, and Bearer is in his familiar black clothes as The Undertaker's manager.

"As I said, Mr. Paul Bearer, you're a decent man, now excuse me while I take care of this creep who desecrates the American flag."

Turturro takes his jacket off and approaches Mr. Fuji, and the spot cuts to the tag page as we hear the sounds of Turturro punching him.

"Oh, and tell The Undertaker I said hello," Turturro says at the end.

Working with Lawrence Taylor, however, scared the living hell out of me.

We had arranged through his agents that Taylor would be needed for one hour, two at the most, to cut promos on Bam Bam Bigelow, his opponent at WrestleMania. The great LT, a Hall of Fame linebacker with the New York Giants, was booked in an exquisite suite in a fancy hotel in Florida, and I had an adjacent room where we would set up a gray background drape and light the room before the shoot, which was scheduled for noon. I wanted to make this as simple as could be for the legendary linebacker. Little did I know this luxurious hotel had a golf course, too.

Noon came and passed on the day of the shoot without Lawrence Taylor appearing. At one o'clock he was still a no-show. At two I knocked on his door. No answer. So I called his agent.

"He's not there?" the agent asked.

"No, he is not."

"Does the hotel have a golf course?"

"Yes, it does."

"That explains it. I'll call him now."

"Thank you."

A half hour later Taylor stormed into my hotel room, where the set was ready and the production lights were on. Anger and aggression seeped from every pore of his being.

"Who's in charge here?" he demanded.

"I am, Mr. Taylor."

He angrily pulled me aside from the crew before continuing.

"Do you know who the fuck I am?" he said as he guided me into the bathroom to talk privately. Sweat was pouring down his face and his nose was running. Taylor was enraged and ready for physical combat in that moment.

"Yes I do, Mr. Taylor."

"Then why the fuck would you pull me off the golf course to come here?" he shouted.

"Because I was worried," I replied, my body shaking.

"Do you know who the fuck I am? I can destroy you in a second, you little man."

"I'm sorry," I said in a passive way to offset his aggression. "We were scheduled to do this shoot at noon and I was concerned. It will take less than an hour, I promise."

He backed off. His voice was still angry, but now he wasn't as loud.

"So you had to pull me off the fucking golf course as I was playing a round with my friends?"

"I just called your agent. I was concerned. *He* pulled you off the course."

Taylor sighed and took a deep breath. He was calm now.

"Okay, let's do this."

"Let me get you a wet towel and a tissue to cool you down and clean your nose."

"Thank you," he said. He wiped his face, walked onto the set, and in forty-five minutes we were done.

In that earlier moment I literally feared for my life. This athletic freak could have destroyed me in seconds. Thankfully I was able to defuse the anger.

A week later, I saw Taylor training to be a wrestler in a ring set up in the bowels of the WWF studios. When he saw me, he calmly called me over.

"I'm sorry for the way I acted last week," he said. "I just love golf and I forgot we had that shoot."

"It's all good," I said. "We got what we needed to get."

"Yes we did!" he said, flashing a brilliant white smile, and gave me a fist bump.

7

THE MONDAY NIGHT WARS

Monday night, September 4, 1995. It's a night I will never forget.

World Championship Wrestling (WCW) would debut its new show *Nitro* live to the entire world that night on TNT. It was the brainchild of Ted Turner and Eric Bischoff, and it aired at exactly the same time as *Monday Night Raw* on the USA Network. It was WCW's way of saying they were eager to play with the big boys. Judging by the huge crowd and a unique venue, the Mall of America in Minneapolis, MN, it appeared they were ready to, as well. And so the first shot was fired in a war that would last for over three years.

Much has been written about those golden years that revolutionized the world of professional wrestling, so I'll keep my stories to a perspective not yet heard.

At the time, *Raw* was an edited, prerecorded show that would be voiced-over live and in real time by play-by-play announcer Vince McMahon and his color commentator Jerry "The King" Lawler in Stamford. The thought was that we could keep up the illusion that *Raw* was live by talking about current events of the day, hiding the fact that we were taped. *Nitro* was fully live, however. Anything spontaneous, unpredictable and potentially damaging to the WWF could happen. And on that very first night, it did.

I was in Studio One in Stamford that night. On one television screen was our show, on the other WCW's *Nitro*. McMahon and Lawler were in the adjacent audio booth, and through a glass window they could peek at both feeds on the screens in front of us. While we were in a commercial break, the unthinkable happened: Lex Luger, wearing black tights, appeared live on *Nitro*. Jaws dropped in Stamford. No one had a clue this was a possibility. Vince's face turned pale. This invincible man suddenly seemed vulnerable.

Soon to air on *Raw* was a prerecorded match featuring Lex Luger dressed in red, white and blue as the American Hero, a match that was taped days earlier. Forget surprise. Now we were fully exposed for the entire nationwide television audience to see.

How could WCW have pulled this off without anyone at the highest levels of the WWF having even the slightest of clues?

Eric Bischoff would later explain how the secret was kept close to the vest.

"I told Lex Luger, 'Do not stay at the same hotel as the other wrestlers,'" Bischoff recalled. "And 'Do not show up to the arena until about thirty minutes before you are set to appear.'"

What frightened me most at that moment was the feeling I had that this was merely the first of many surprises to come. And it was.

Yes, the WWF maintained its ratings lead for another nine months, but each week WCW *Nitro* was inching closer. To counter, McMahon commissioned me to create the infamous "Billionaire Ted" vignettes, weekly spoofs that would air in each episode of *Raw* in an attempt to diminish what the WCW was all about.

The idea sickened me. Why give the competition credence and recognition in our program? Professionally, I was not happy. It was the saddest six months of my creative life.

At first the Billionaire Ted vignettes were comedic sketches that parodied the media mogul Ted Turner, the owner of World Championship Wrestling. Vince wanted to attack Turner because he didn't want to acknowledge Bischoff in any capacity, even though Bischoff was behind everything WCW was doing. Bischoff was where McMahon's true ire was directed.

By this time, Hulk Hogan and Randy Savage had jumped ship to WCW, so the initial skits mocked Turner by referencing the age of these wrestlers, who we dubbed "The Huckster" and "Nacho Man." The sketches, promoted as "Billionaire Ted's Rasslin' Warroom," were shot in a studio in Stamford and mimicked Turner in his own boardroom trying to copy WWF programming. His older wrestlers would say they were no longer able to do the more athletic moves or use original promotional tactics. A later sketch featured Billionaire Ted wanting to buy some "WWF New Generation" wrestlers, to which a WWF voice-over said, "It's not for sale."

Every week, a sketch aired. And every week, WCW inched closer to the WWF in the ratings. Nothing could stop the inevitable.

Eventually the skits crossed a line, which the USA Network would not tolerate for long. Although the spots were initially popular, they soon became focused on Ted Turner personally. One had Billionaire Ted on a mock trivia game show identifying quotes with racial and sexual language he may have said a decade earlier. Another had Billionaire Ted as a guest on a parody of *Larry King Live*, refusing to answer why The Huckster's salary was drawn from more profitable Turner businesses instead of the loss-making WCW. I had very little to do with the writing of these later spots, which became malicious a few months in, but I still had the detested task of tweaking the scripts, directing the shoots and producing the vignettes. The final spot that aired on USA featured Billionaire Ted in front of a Federal Trade Commission committee in a parody of the iconic scene from the movie *A Few Good Men*, with the famous line "You can't handle the truth!"

Thankfully, USA Network president Kay Koplovitz put an end to them. She felt that stress had gotten the better of McMahon, and that although the skits were humorous at first, they had now become mean-spirited. She was right. "Thank you Kay!" I said to myself.

On a podcast decades later, Eric Bischoff revealed to wrestling promoter Conrad Thompson that he was told that Turner was actually amused by the Billionaire Ted vignettes. They made him laugh rather than rile him up.

Vince, however, would try to have the final word. At WrestleMania XII, live on pay-per-view, the final skit — free from the constraints of the USA Network — culminated in a match between The Huckster and Nacho Man, with Billionaire Ted acting as the referee. In the end, all three died of heart attacks.

I have one word to say about that: reprehensible.

Our reign as king of the hill would end shortly thereafter. On May 5, 1996, Scott Hall joined WCW. A month later, on June 10, Kevin Nash joined as well. Finally the WCW took the ratings lead, and *Nitro* became the top-rated show on all of cable television. It would remain there for an incredible eighty-three straight weeks. In the eyes of wrestling fans, the behemoth that was the WWF had been reduced to secondary status.

A few weeks later, Vince convened a small group of his most trusted production heads to explain how to counter the departures of Razor Ramon and Kevin Nash.

"Guys, Razor Ramon and Diesel are just characters, like Batman and Superman," McMahon said. "They are not real people. We can replace them with other athletes to play their roles."

So we created the "Fake Razor," played by Rick Bognar, and the "Fake Diesel" as portrayed by Glenn Jacobs (who would later gain fame as Kane). But the idea was preposterous.

Both of them lacked the charisma and the palpable air of arrogance of the characters they'd tried to replace. They looked like adults wearing Halloween costumes, and the audience frowned upon the whole idea. Professional wrestling may be fake in their minds, but this was just fraud. They were insulted. And so they booed, but not in a good way, not because these were bad-guy characters. Their boos were of deep disgust. They didn't want to see this crap.

Not only had we lost the ratings war to WCW, but we were in a free fall that would nearly put the WWF out of business.

Weeks after that fiasco, McMahon gathered a half dozen or so of his top creative people together in a hastily arranged meeting at the studios in Stamford.

"Guys," he began, sounding like a defeated emperor, "we are hemorrhaging money. We are getting our butts kicked by WCW. We have to make a change. I don't know what that is, but if we don't come up with something we may be out of business soon."

Everyone in the room was solemn. Vince was dead serious. Many had heard rumors that in order to make payroll, he'd needed to take a loan out of Titan Towers, a building McMahon personally owned and "rented" to the WWF.

But I had an idea . . .

Backstage with EC3, who had one of the catchiest entrance themes ever.

BELOW: Pre-show in London, England, with announcer Josh Mathews.

Kurt Angle in London, England, on his TNA farewell tour.

RIGHT: "The Charismatic Enigma" Jeff Hardy, one of my all-time favorites.

Thank goodness The Undertaker did not give me a tombstone piledriver!

BELOW: Vince McMahon painted as the devil for the first "King of the Ring" commercial.

Myself, Chris Chambers and a member of the pyrotechnics team.

Working with Billy Corgan of Smashing Pumpkins fame was a pleasure.

BELOW: Directing Ric Flair's Last Match, one of the highlights of my career.

Catching up with Mick Foley backstage at Ric Flair's Last Match.

Getting a little love with the wonderful Karen Jarrett backstage.

"Double J" Jeff Jarrett, one of the greatest bosses/friends to work with.

"The Nature Boy" Ric Flair on the set of his final match.

When I'm off, I like to throw down a beer . . . or three!

It was always my pleasure to serve as footstool for the lovely Velvet Sky.

8

THE ATTITUDE ERA

One could make the case that if David Sahadi had never joined the WWF in the fall of 1992, the boom of the mid-to-late nineties never would have happened and the world of sports entertainment and professional wrestling would have sunk into the muck of obscurity and irrelevance.

Yet that would be arrogant of me to say. And also a lie. It would still be around, but perhaps in another form.

The truth is there was originally a "Core Four" that had a vision and planted the seeds of a dream that would become the Attitude Era: Kevin Dunn, Chris Chambers, Jim Johnston and myself. Then suddenly a fifth — the young, creative and energetic Adam Pennucci. And then Vince Russo started writing an edgier show.

The funny thing is there was never a grand plan, blueprint or shared vision among the creative, production and corporate departments at first. All these little things began organically and individually, first with production and image spots, and then everything coalesced and all our ideas seamlessly merged into one. It was synchronicity and serendipity at their finest.

Coming from the world of NBC Sports, I brought a real sports mentality to how the WWF superstars would be showcased. And I presented them as real athletes, capable of amazing athletic feats, rather than the cartoonish characters that by this time were getting stale.

The first-ever spot that introduced the new Attitude logo and launched this amazing era was filmed in an abandoned warehouse in Connecticut and featured a dozen top WWF superstars. Amid the rubble, the muscular athletes looked like the mythical gods of Athens, phoenixes rising from the aftermath of destruction. They stared into the camera with conviction and determination. They didn't speak, but we heard their thoughts in their own voices, which were recorded separately and dropped in during the edit. Here is the copy, written with the help and creativity of Chris Chambers, that would define everything we did thereafter:

"I know what you're thinking . . ."

"I'm not a real athlete."

"I'm just a 'wrestler.'"

"I'm six foot ten, 328 pounds. I was a consensus All-American at Florida State."

"I was a linebacker for the Dallas Cowboys."

"My jersey was retired at Florida State."

"I was the first-ever Ultimate Fighting Champion."

"When you step through those ropes, bad things happen."

"I had over two hundred stitches."

"I've broken bones."

"I had a dozen concussions."

"I nearly broke my neck."

"Separated shoulders."

"Blown-out knees."

"But I still got up."

"This is who I am."

"This is what I do."

"I'm not really an athlete?"

"This isn't real?"

"Try lacing my boots."

When we first presented the concept to Vince McMahon, he didn't like it at all. When he left the room, Kevin Dunn turned to me.

"Shoot it anyway, David," Dunn said. "He'll like it when he sees it."

Dunn, as usual, was right. He was undoubtedly McMahon's most trusted ally, and he knew Vince well. When Vince saw the spot a week later, he instantly loved it.

That single spot — with the new "scratch" logo, created on a napkin — started a domino effect that would ripple through every level of the WWF: creative, production, sales, digital media, you name it. A seed was planted, and soon a forest would emerge.

Vince Russo and the creative team began thinking outside the box. They pushed the envelope when others were too timid, afraid of change. And everyone at the WWF fed off that and felt empowered again. We had devised a strategic counterattack. The entire product became edgy. The storylines were now very believable, and often real. The shows, from beginning to end, felt like a train wreck waiting to happen, and often it did. And that was so exciting because the line was now blurred between what was real and what was contrived. The Attitude Era saved the WWF from bankruptcy because at the time the company was in dire financial straits and losing the Monday Night War to the competition.

Three months after we debuted the first Attitude spot, I decided to do a sequel. The concept was a passing of the torch from wrestlers of previous eras to the new generation of superstars. It featured Hall of Famers Classy Freddie Blassie, Ernie Ladd, Killer Kowalski, Pat Patterson and Gorilla Monsoon. It was shot in an abandoned gymnasium in Troy, New York, just beyond the shadows of Albany. A ring was placed on the gym floor, the ropes sagging to represent age and a bygone era. The spot was shot in black and white to add to the nostalgic feel. Jim Johnston wrote a melancholy track of original music that felt perfectly attuned to the black-and-white imagery.

Freddie Blassie is the first legend seen in the spot. He slowly takes a seat alone in the balcony above the ring.

"I can still hear the echoes cheering my name," Blassie says, and the other legends soon join in:

"Time cannot silence the crowd."

"I never did a moonsault."

"Nor walked the top rope."

"We never flew through the air."

"We were men of courage."

"Men of steel."

"They are men without fear."

"I can still hear the echoes cheering my name," says Ernie Ladd, standing in the dilapidated ring and waving to a crowd dressed in fifties-era clothing and cheering from the balcony above. Then we cut back to a tight shot of Ladd with a tear running down his face before returning to the shot of him waving, the crowd now gone.

"But today, I cheer for them," Blassie says, as the spot ends and the crane shot lowers, as if Blassie is rising to heaven.

During filming I received a call from Kevin Dunn.

"David, Vince just called and asked, 'What the hell is Sahadi doing shooting a commercial with the old-timers in Albany? We are about the new generation now.'

"I said, 'Vince, I don't know the exact concept, but Sahadi has a pretty good track record here so I'm sure it's going to be good.'"

It better be, Vince told Dunn before hanging up.

"It will be great," I reassured Dunn.

"I'm sure it will. I have faith in you."

"Thank you. And Vince will love it when he sees it."

Four days later, the spot was edited, mixed, and the tag page was added. It was a finished product. Dunn informed Vince, and in just minutes McMahon came to the studio to see it. Unlike the premiere of the first *Raw* open years earlier, I made sure Jim Johnston, the master of music who wrote and produced nearly every entrance theme for the WWF superstars, had the volume turned up high so that Vince could feel the emotion of the spot.

With Vince were his son Shane and Pat Patterson. McMahon's arms were crossed in a way that made one think he was not happy and was expecting to dislike the spot. Then Vince said just two words.

"Play it."

And so it played. Ten seconds in, Vince said, "Oh god."

Five seconds later, "Dammit." Then another "Oh god."

Then he suddenly left the audio suite before the tag page came up.

I was nervous. He hated it, I thought. I turned my head to Shane. Shane was smiling.

"Shane, what does that mean?" I asked.

"You got him, Sahadi!" he said with joy as he patted my back. "You got him."

I walked out of the studio. There on the cold concrete floor just outside the door sat Vince, sobbing hysterically. He looked up when he saw me and shook my hand.

"Thank you," he said. "Thank you." He was still sobbing.

I walked upstairs to Dunn's office and shared the good news.

"Kevin, the spot made Vince cry. He is crying right now on the concrete floor outside the studio."

Dunn smiled. "I can't wait to see it."

On my way back downstairs to the production studios, there was Vince, now sitting on the stairs and still crying. Patterson and Shane were by his side consoling him.

"Thank you," Vince said once again. "Thank you."

It took me a year or so to understand why the spot affected Vince so much. Then I realized he probably felt it on a personal level. To me and everyone else, the spot was about a passing of the torch from the stars of then to the superstars of now. To Vince, I believe, it was a passing of the torch from his father, Vince McMahon Sr., to him. He realized how he had taken his father's vision to heights that back in the day one could not have imagined.

A month later I had an idea for another spot. The first two were huge successes, so I wanted to make it a trilogy. The third spot would come full circle.

This production featured images of kids between the ages of seven and twelve. It was shot outdoors on a sunny day, the complete opposite of the "Legends" spot, which had a dark and dreary look. Railroad tracks, barns, fields of corn and highway overpasses were the background locations. And we shot them in the sunshine to symbolize the bright light of a future generation of wrestling stars emerging. The imagery represented youth, hope, vibrance, and the start of an evolution of sorts.

The spot was edited to jump from one kid to the next, and the copy was rebellious and defiant. It epitomized the vibe of the Attitude Era.

"I don't want to be a doctor."

"A lawyer."

"A businessman."

"A car salesman."

"I don't want to be who you want me to be."

"I want to be a rebel."

"A leader."

"A champion."

"A pioneer."

"A star who captivates the attention of the world."

"I don't want to be who you want me to be."

"Or what others may wish."

"I want to be me."

"I want to be free."

When the spot was finished four days later, I literally had goosebumps on both forearms. The message was powerful and purposeful. These defiant kids came across as being strong, bold adults, symbolizing WWF superstars in their infancy, before they would ever put on tights or enter a wrestling ring.

The following week Dunn brought the spot to Titan Towers for Vince and nearly a dozen corporate executives to see. I was sure it would be a home run and strike an emotional chord in the deepest chambers of their hearts. The first two spots did. This new one certainly tugged at their hearts, but instead of a home run it ended up being a pop-up to the pitcher's mound.

"They do not want to air that spot," Dunn told me after the viewing.

"Why?" I asked. "It's powerful and sends a great message of being your own person, not someone who is molded by society or even their parents."

"I know, David. And I personally love it. But it made some of the men in the room emotional."

"Well that's good, right?"

"Yes, but although most in the room liked it, a tiny few got teary-eyed, so the minority overruled the majority."

"Tell me why?"

"One said, 'I want my son to be a businessman when he grows up.' Then another said, 'I want my son to be just like me.' And a third one said, 'I don't want my son to grow up being a rebel.'"

"Kevin, they are missing the message. Rebels change the world, often for the better. The personal egos and inflated opinions of these corporate suits are what killed it. Admit it."

"I know," Dunn replied. "But unfortunately they refuse to allow us to air the spot. It is what it is."

In the fall of that year, I nonetheless submitted the spot to the Promax Gold Medallion Awards, with the caveat that the spot had not aired yet, but hopefully one day it would. The spot was recognized with a Silver Medallion Award, a second-place trophy to the gold. I was happy. Again, it was validation.

Although I could not complete the trifecta, the spot was still a success because it inspired the hundred-plus employees in production who saw it. It inspired them to view everything we did in a different light, to tap into their inner youth, to raise their aspirations higher than ever imagined. To delve into new frontiers never before known.

As a whole, the Attitude Era made us all think outside the box, while the old guard was clinging to old, tired formulas. We were the new generation, determined to take risks instead of clinging fearfully to safety. We shunned fear. We embraced hope. We believed in our new vision, and everyone fed off that.

No one can doubt that the Attitude Era saved the WWF from bankruptcy. The financial picture was bad at the time; we were getting our asses kicked by *Nitro*. The early days of the Attitude Era were the start of our remarkable awakening and resurgence. Each week, each month, we kept pushing the envelope, crossing lines and getting edgier. Success was inevitable, and after eighty-three weeks of losing the ratings war to WCW, we finally took the lead for good in 1998. For nearly a decade after, WWE would be the number one–rated weekly show in all of cable television.

No other show came close.

No other show can say that to this day.

9

THE SUPER BOWL COMMERCIAL

"We are buying a thirty-second commercial spot in the Super Bowl," Kevin Dunn told me in the fall of 1998. "And we are not hiring an ad agency. *You* are the ad agency."

I was both thrilled and anxious. Feelings of joy and fear were mixed with a myriad of emotions. I knew this spot would be seen by over 100 million viewers. The company had put their trust in me, and I didn't want to disappoint.

"So come up with something really special," Dunn continued. "Give us your best."

I was determined to do so. I was inspired. And I decided to trust my hopes, not my fears.

A week later we held a meeting in the executive conference room to pitch my idea with everyone important present, anyone who had a voice that Vince would listen to, an opinion he would respect. About a dozen people were there. They were excited to hear the creative vision I'd conceived.

The idea was a total satire, an obvious spoof — of ourselves. Self-deprecating humor is something I've always admired, and I often use it myself. My concept was to have Vince McMahon play the role of the emperor of this evil empire, spewing lies with a smile as he walks the hallways of Titan Towers, smiling while saying how wonderful and benign our brand of entertainment was. It would be as if he was the devil tempting Eve to take a bite of the forbidden apple in our Garden of Eden, the corporate offices.

As Vince strolls through the halls praising our virtues, wrestlers would be seen in the background being calm and civil while the WWF employees are the unruly ones, fighting each other like mad dogs. Many had a negative opinion of the violence we passed off as entertainment, and we turned the narrative upside down.

When I finished my pitch, Vince smiled. He liked it. Most of the others did as well. Vince Russo, however, suggested one slight tweak, and it was a game changer. It took the idea to a higher level.

"I love the concept," Russo said, "but why not have the wrestlers be the superstars of this spot, the spokesmen, and not Vince?"

"Great idea," remarked another executive.

"Yes it is," said another.

I couldn't have agreed more, and immediately altered the script accordingly.

The finished spot opens with a quick establishing shot of the exterior of Titan Towers, the corporate offices. Then we cut inside as wrestlers, in full ring gear, walk around the offices and hallways of real, everyday employees while singing our praises and virtues.

"Most people have the wrong impression of the World Wrestling Federation," Stone Cold says as he strolls through the lobby of the executive floor. "We are a nonviolent form of entertainment."

Then out of nowhere he nails an employee with a stiff chair shot to the back.

"We never use sex to enhance our image," Sable then says, though she's dressed seductively in black leather, and employees all around her are engaging in sensual acts.

"As athletes," The Rock says, removing his sunglasses as he walks down a hall, "we understand the importance of being positive role models." As he says this a brawl is unfolding in a conference room beside him, and an employee throws a co-worker through a glass window into the hall just behind him. The Rock never flinches.

"We are good, wholesome family entertainment," The Undertaker declares as he calmly steps out of an elevator, oblivious to the bedlam around him — including the absurdity of a blind referee navigating his way through the melee with a walking stick.

"We are just trying to make the world a better place for mankind," adds Mick Foley, sitting calmly on the upper balcony above the main lobby, where the employee fights devolve into complete chaos and brutality.

"WWF Attitude," says the deep, booming voice of Jim Fagan, our top voice-over artist, as the tag page appears on the screen.

Then we cut back to Vince McMahon for a final shot outside the towers as an employee gets thrown from the top floor.

"Get it?" Vince says.

The spot was voted the fifth-best Super Bowl commercial in *Ad Age* magazine. It gave the company worldwide prominence and me personal validation.

"The satirical theme of the video was brilliant," remarked Peter Fitzpatrick, a wrestling columnist, "as wrestlers talked about the WWF being wholesome and family-friendly, nonviolent entertainment while all hell broke loose all around them."

Almost all of the commercials that aired during the game were conceived by ad agencies and produced for millions of dollars by production companies. The cost for our spot was less than $200,000. It wasn't because Vince was frugal; I have no doubt he would have spent millions if needed. It's just that Vince had such high regard for our entire production team and knew no advertising company could conceive and produce a better creative spot with high production values than us.

"The concept of this spot is fantastic," The Rock said during one of his many interviews on the set. "It fits the WWF to a T. It is WWF Attitude personified. It's balls to the walls. It's madness, it's mayhem, it's the whole spectrum."

The two-day shoot was not without some truly scary moments, however.

In the very first take with The Rock, a stuntman was thrown through "candy glass" but had a bad landing. Even though he was padded top to bottom underneath his suit for protection, a one-inch gap between his lower back and rear end hit the decorative trim of the wall outside.

"Help!" he screamed in pain. "I need help! I can't feel my legs."

The paramedics on hand immediately rushed to his aid. At first we feared he might be paralyzed from the waist down.

I was devastated. Immediately, I stopped the shoot. My concern was with his health, a person I had never met before this day. A person with a family and a future ahead of him.

Nearly an hour passed. I called an early lunch break for the crew. Then Drew Jiritano, our stunt coordinator, gathered a few of us in an office to talk.

"We are sending him to the hospital for an analysis," he said. "David, were you happy with that one take?" I wasn't. It was just the first of a few I wanted to perfect.

"No," I replied. "The Rock's timing was a bit off, but if the stuntman is really hurt that bad then we will live with that one take and —"

"David, I don't mean to sound cold and uncaring, but he's a stuntman," Drew said, interrupting me mid-sentence, his voice filled with conviction.

"He knows it's a dangerous business. We do everything we possibly can to protect them, but they know there's always a slight inherent risk of danger. So let's continue. I have a replacement. The show must go on." And so, with heavy hearts, we went on. (It turned out the stuntman wasn't seriously injured.)

On the second day, we had another miscue. It was the final scene, shot on street level outside Titan Towers, where a stuntman disguised as an employee gets thrown out of the window and plummets five stories. The stuntman was a bit nervous before the first take.

"This is definitely high up," he said. "And the airbag looks small."

Jiritano tried to ease his nerves.

"It's not," Jiritano said. "It looks that way because we're high up, but you'll be fine."

Unfortunately, the stuntman wouldn't be. Little did we know when Jiritano spoke that our first take would be our final take.

For those who don't know, what's known as candy glass — easily breakable — is not what is used in high-end stunts. It was the real glass of the building, thick and strong like the windshield of a car. Small explosives were strategically placed around all four sides of the window, and it was up to the stunt coordinator to detonate them at the precise moment that the stuntman, who would get a running start from about ten feet away, was about to crash into it. As the stuntman was pacing around with deep breaths seconds before the shoot, I yelled "Roll camera," and the stuntman made the sign of the cross.

"Here goes," Jiritano shouted. "Three . . . two . . . one . . . *go!*"

The glass exploded as the stuntman jumped through, but the tip of his foot caught on a tiny piece of the metal insert that held the window in place. Instead of doing a 180 and landing flat on his back on the giant cushion that was out of sight of the camera angle, he spun in free fall and landed on his head.

Fortunately, the stuntman wasn't seriously hurt, but his head was woozy and he seemed disoriented. I decided to send him to the hospital as a precautionary measure. That would be the only take we would do that day.

When all was said and done, that spot gave me greater status, and a prestigious award as well. But what mattered most to me was that it made the world see us in a different light. It proved we were the kings of entertainment. It made the company proud.

That spot was written and produced for a huge mainstream audience, most of whom did not watch WWF programming at the time. The very next night on *Monday Night Raw*, we aired a similar, alternative piece that was meant for our fans only.

"Last night the WWF aired a spot in the Super Bowl that was well received," says Jerry Lawler. "But the WWF superstars also had fun and spoofed themselves with outtakes that were never meant to be seen, until now. Here's the spot that didn't air."

The spot was identical, except that the lines and background scenes were changed.

"Most people have the right impression about the WWF," Stone Cold Steve Austin proudly proclaims. "We *are* a violent form of entertainment."

"We *always* use sex to promote our image," the sensuous Sable says, the background scenes even more salacious than before.

"As athletes," The Rock adds, "we could give a monkey's ass about being positive role models."

"We are *not* wholesome family entertainment," The Undertaker declares.

"We don't give a damn about mankind," says Mick Foley, also known as "Mankind."

Our audience laughed at our satire of a satire.

Little did I know, some people in production were not laughing at all. Somehow, for reasons unknown, those two spots would also create some jealous adversaries in my working world.

10

THE SUPER BOWL SPOT THAT NEVER AIRED

After the success and critical acclaim of the initial Super Bowl commercial, the WWF decided to buy not one but three spots the following year. Two would air during the pregame show, and the third — the payoff — during the actual game. Once again, I was tasked with conceiving, writing and directing the three spots.

The WWF was already hugely successful. Now we were seeking respect. The lead actor in the third spot would be the man who "never got respect anywhere," the legendary comedian Rodney Dangerfield.

What were we going to do with Dangerfield? We were going to kill him in the third spot. On national television, before a worldwide audience, during the most-watched event of the year. It would shock people. How dare we? I could visualize the headline: "WWF kills Rodney Dangerfield in Super Bowl commercial." This would garner major headlines everywhere, and the attention of the world, whether the spot was loved or hated. That I knew deep in my soul. Being noticed, and remembered, is the main point of any commercial campaign.

I was given a budget of $500,000, nearly three times that of the previous Super Bowl commercial. The two spots leading up to the Dangerfield ad would feature our top talent pleasantly going household to household in typical suburban neighborhoods in an attempt to gain respect.

The tagline — "We are just trying to gain respect, one household at a time" — would be delivered by Vince McMahon himself at the end.

Because of the schedule of our live events, the spot with Dangerfield would be shot a week beforehand while all of the WWF superstars were in Los Angeles shooting *Raw* live, then taping an episode of *SmackDown* the following day. The set was on an iconic soundstage at Paramount Studios in Hollywood, a legendary facility where many of the great classics of the forties and fifties were filmed.

Of course, being the WWF, we always loved to poke fun at ourselves, so the initial spots would start out cordial but quickly devolve into complete chaos.

One spot would unfold like this. Stone Cold is standing outside the white front door of a quaint suburban home. A housewife opens the door, and with a polite smile he says, "Hello, I'm Stone Cold Steve Austin." The woman abruptly frowns and slams the door in Austin's face.

Feeling disrespected, another WWF superstar suddenly dives through a window and spears her unsuspecting husband, who was eating breakfast at the kitchen table. Another bursts through a wall and clotheslines his wife onto the floor. A third breaks through a wooden floor and chases a child out of the house, and another puts the family dog in a submission hold. Then we cut to McMahon, smiling in a serene setting of evergreen trees, who delivers the tagline: "We are just trying to gain respect, one household at a time." A giant crane rises for a wide shot of the madness unfolding on the suburban streets beyond the trees. Houses are ablaze, and police cars are racing to the scene with sirens blasting as dozens of residents run frantically for their lives — all while being chased around by WWF superstars dressed in their ring gear.

The second spot was just a slight variation on the first. Both could be shot in a single day, if carefully planned and scheduled, after we filmed the spot with Dangerfield.

We hired top-notch crews to build a mansion at the Paramount soundstage to serve as Dangerfield's home for the spot, and it took over two weeks, including all the small but intricate, crucial details. My producer was again Dave "Derk" Anderko, and he enlisted Hollywood's finest crews possible. One crew was the special effects team from the Academy Award–winning movie *Armageddon*. A separate company built an elaborate miniature model of Dangerfield's mansion, which would be used for the final shot.

To stay true to the theme of the first two spots, this one would start with a shot of Vince McMahon, at night, knocking on the door of the mansion.

"Hello Rodney," Vince would say with a smile when the door opened.

"Get lost!" Dangerfield would exclaim, slamming the door in Vince's face. Then we'd cut back to a shot of McMahon, angry as hell, his face reddening and eyes nearly bulging out of their sockets.

"Get him, boys!" McMahon would then command.

Suddenly, a group of angry WWF superstars would storm the mansion, breaking through windows, walls, ceilings and floors, each one hell-bent on delivering their signature finishing moves on the legendary comedian (who would obviously be played by a stuntman).

The set was so elaborate that electrical sparks would flash when walls were broken, plaster dust would drift through each room, and pieces of wood would fall from the ceilings each time Dangerfield took a major bump. A dog, which Rodney insisted on being in the shoot, would sit quietly amid the chaos, eventually covering its eyes with its paws instead of even trying to save its owner. Then we'd cut to the tag page before going back to Vince and Kane standing outside the mansion.

"Finish the job," McMahon would command Kane. The Big Red Monster would then raise his arms as the miniature model of the house exploded in flames. Yes, Rodney Dangerfield would be killed on global television.

I keep saying "would" while describing these spots because they were never filmed.

Just two days before the shoot, walking the set in Los Angeles and giving my final tidbits of advice, I received a devastating call from Kevin Dunn.

"David, the shoot is dead."

"What? You're joking, right?"

"No, I am not."

"Why?"

"Someone got into Vince's ear and said we should air a spot of all of our positive press clippings over the past year instead."

"Press clippings?" I said in disbelief. "Really? Press clippings?"

"Yes. And other pictures that boast about our success."

"That is so wrong." I was adamant. "This is the Super Bowl. People want to be entertained by the commercials, not 'informed' by press clippings and a voice-over describing how successful we are now."

"Sorry. It's killed."

"Kevin, we already paid nearly $485,000 of the half-million-dollar budget to construct these sets for this commercial. The talent is already in town. Let's just shoot it anyway since it's basically already paid for."

"No chance. End of conversation."

To this day I'm not sure who convinced McMahon to go in a different direction. It could have been Stone Cold, The Rock, Mankind or any of the top stars that had Vince's ear at the time. It remains a mystery.

Days later, I convinced Dunn that a spot that featured press clippings would suck. Big time.

"Well, you have less than a week to come up with another concept," Dunn said. "We have to run everything by standards and practices at the network, and that's our final deadline for our creative submission, or we will lose those three spots."

"I will," I replied, bitterness still evident in my voice. "They won't be as good or as grand, but I will."

The three spots I quickly conceived were again parodies, but all separate concepts.

The first shows elderly people in a nursing home snoozing at midday, approximately the same time the spot would air. As the clock strikes three, three bells are heard as if it was the start of a match. Suddenly they awaken, energized, and the elderly people mimic WWF wrestlers, hitting each other with bedpans and canes while shouting the signature catchphrases of our top superstars.

The second was set in a maternity ward at a hospital with two nurses checking on the newbies. Suddenly one newborn farts. The nurses look at each other in shock before realizing it came from one of the babies. Then the newborns, dressed as various WWF wrestlers, start quoting our catchphrases as the nurses flee the room in panic.

The main commercial, which aired during the game, was a spoof on a beauty pageant. It was called "Miss Congeniality" and featured Jim Fagan, the announcer I employed at NBC Sports then covertly at the WWF, as the on-camera host of this event. Fagan, dressed in a tuxedo, had the look as well as the voice. When the runner-up, from Connecticut, was not chosen the winner, a brawl between the female contestants broke out.

"What's happening to my pageant?" Fagan said in disgust.

The first commercial never aired, except on WWF television. The American Association of Retired Persons found it "offensive," and the network succumbed to their complaints. So instead the hospital spot, the least creative of the three, aired twice. But the beauty pageant spoof, which aired during the game, was critically acclaimed.

Here's what *Ad Age* magazine had to say the following day:

"A faux beauty pageant advertises a fake sport during the country's biggest sporting event, one marked that year by a preponderance of dot-com advertisers. It was a dissonant moment for viewers, perhaps. But a successful one, too, by some measures. Nine of the ten websites with the most traffic after Super Bowl XXXIX [sic] were dot-coms, according to a study by Media Metrix. The other was WWF.com."

Yes, it made the top ten most successful spots of the Super Bowl that year, but I wasn't happy. Yes, I garnered another Promax Gold Medallion Award, another on my way to twenty-seven, but personal acclaim did not bring satisfaction. I cared about the company first and foremost. And to this day I'm still convinced the original concept featuring Rodney Dangerfield would have been in the top five, and probably the top three.

We never killed Rodney Dangerfield on national TV during the Super Bowl. If we had, the headlines and buzz it would have generated the next day would have been incredible.

11

AGGRESSION: THE MUSIC VIDEOS

On March 21, 2001, the WWF released a soundtrack album called *WWF Aggression*. The album featured the entrance theme music of our top superstars re-recorded by various hip-hop artists, such as Run-DMC, Snoop Dogg, Method Man, Redman and Mystikal.

The album instantly became a commercial success. It reached number eight on the US Billboard 200. In Canada it hit number six. It also reached number ten in the R&B/hip-hop category. It was straight-ahead hardcore rap. It had an edge, and that's why I loved it.

I was tasked with shooting the first music video for the album. It was titled "Know Your Role" and featured The Rock and Method Man.

By this time The Rock was becoming a mainstream celebrity. He wasn't one just yet, but he was soon to sign a contract to star in his first movie, *The Scorpion King*. My concept for this video was to make him seem as if he already was a Hollywood megastar.

We filmed The Rock in time-lapse scenes driving an exotic black Ferrari through the chic streets of South Beach, Miami, a very trendy spot at the time. It was where every celebrity came to hang out and vacation in its heyday. In the video were shots of Miss Millennium 2000, interior scenes of the hottest nightclubs in South Beach, and beautiful women who fawned over The Rock whenever he walked through a posh club. Men looked on in envy of the attention he was getting.

The night before the shoot, I beheld a beautiful exotic dancer on Ocean Drive, just outside my hotel, bringing a sensual seductiveness to the colorful, neon-lit streets. I approached and asked for her phone number. She obliged when I told her why, and I hired her for $500 to dance alone in an abandoned hotel the next day as part of this video. It was an idea that came to me in the moment. My most creative visions always found me when I wasn't looking.

The next day we filmed the dancer in the abandoned hotel. It was just a few blocks away from the glamour of Ocean Drive, but it felt like we were in a foreign country. We weren't given permission to shoot there because there was no one around to ask permission from. So we were clandestine and used minimal lighting for this shoot so that no one would notice. We were in and out that afternoon in less than two hours.

What I loved most about this location was that each room, though roughly the same size, had a different vibe and color. One room was painted in pastel pink, another vivid green and a third aqua blue. Paint chips were peeling from each room, symbolic of a distant time that once was vibrant, but long since forgotten.

A week earlier, when I'd told The Rock about the concept for the video, he was made aware it would be shot at nighttime — from dusk to dawn, eight straight hours without a break — because that was when South Beach glowed at its finest. He didn't complain. He knew it would help his character and enhance his celebrity, even if it required him to stay awake for eight straight hours in the darkness of night.

It was a two-day shoot. On the first day, we filmed beautiful girls in an array of nightclubs as well as the exotic dancer in the abandoned hotel, and added some time-lapse scenics of South Beach at night. Method Man was also scheduled to be there on the first night, but he was a no-show. So I called the production studios in Stamford and they sent me footage of Method Man recording the song in a studio a month earlier. I used that footage of Method Man and projected it on the walls of the warehouse and hotels, and even as a few background shots behind The Rock the next day, to weave him into the video and convince the viewer that he was there as well.

It was a fun shoot, and when I returned to Stamford two days later and edited the video, I was approached by Jim Johnston, one of the many producers on the album.

"David, that is not the best song on the album," Johnston said, "but that music video is amazing and took that song to a higher level."

A day later, when I showed it to Vince McMahon, he disagreed.

"Where is the violence?" Vince asked. "All I take from that video is a good-looking, well-dressed man walking through nightclubs trying to get some pussy."

"He looks like a star," Kevin Dunn countered.

"And that's what I was hoping to accomplish," I added. "I wanted to present him as a Hollywood superstar who gets everyone's attention. I didn't think violence was needed in this video."

"He's not a Hollywood movie star," Vince said. "Not yet anyway."

"Soon he will be," I replied. "So let's make him appear to be a Hollywood star before he even becomes one."

Vince thought for a bit, then reluctantly acquiesced. But I can tell he wasn't happy. He still wanted to see violence.

The next music video we produced was the song "The Kings," performed by Run-DMC and featuring D-Generation X. Initially the video was assigned to another producer, but just a few days before the shoot I was tasked to produce and direct it, as well as come up with a brand new concept. I was given just one day to conceive it. That was a tall task.

But I didn't need a day, it turned out. The creative vision came easily and instantly. Vince wanted violence in the first video, so I was determined to shoot this one with violence fully unleashed. Ruthless aggression at its core. Fire, explosions, riots, the smashing of cars with baseball bats and a sledgehammer? Bring it!

The concept would entail a riot on the streets while Run-DMC was performing the song nearby in a decrepit underground building, which had three levels that we overflowed with grunge and gangsta rap fans in a mad frenzy. The newly signed tag team the Hardy Boyz would be among the fans, too. Jeff Hardy even did a Swanton dive from the third level onto a one-inch crash pad below. I cautioned him not to do it because there wasn't enough padding to prevent a possible injury, but he insisted. It was his idea, so I allowed him one take and one take only. On his own, he did two.

Since pyrotechnics, exploding fireballs and Molotov cocktails would be involved, the video would be shot at night on an abandoned loading dock in Red Bank, New Jersey. The location had a post-apocalyptic feel.

The three members of Run-DMC arrived in a black stretch limousine three hours late. After the no-show by Method Man, I'd anticipated this might be a possibility. When the limousine stopped, the driver got out and summoned me to the car. He opened the back door and there was Reverend Run. The music legend asked me to come in and take a seat beside him, and then the door was closed.

"What is the concept of this video?" Run asked.

"Mayhem and violence," I replied, "but you and D-Generation X are the masters of this apocalyptic future. You are literally the kings of this degenerative domain."

"Can I see a script?"

"Did you not get one? We sent scripts to you and your agents three days ago."

"I never got one."

So I handed him mine. He read it for a minute and was skeptical.

"Why is there violence and why are we attacking the police?"

"You are not attacking the police, you are attacking their cars."

"Why would we do that?"

"The characters of D-Generation X rebel against authority. All sorts of authority. In the end you meet up with D-Generation X and make peace with the police, and they also join in the anarchy."

"Hmm . . ." he sighed, still not convinced.

I tried again. "This video is all about rebelling against authority, at any age and any place, and it has a happy ending."

He was still doubtful. Then he asked one favor.

"When you shoot me singing, make sure you get a tight shot of my face, okay?"

"I promise you I will."

"Look at me," he said, his voice now sterner as he leaned his face into mine. "I want you to shoot my face."

"I will. You have my word."

An hour later we stopped filming the mayhem on the streets with the extras to shoot Reverend Run performing the song amid a sea of frenetic fans. We set the camera atop a dolly that had a 360-degree track so that the background would always be in motion.

One thing I learned over the years when it comes to filming a performer lip-syncing to a track is it always takes three or four takes to get them comfortable and fully immersed in the groove. I planned on shooting Run's face on the third take. The first take was extremely wide, wider than head to toe. I informed Jam Master Jay of my reasoning for this and he fully understood.

"Good plan," Jam said. "I feel you."

"Thank you."

The first take was filmed. I immediately wanted to shoot another, so I told my camera operator to quickly change lenses so that we could start shooting tighter shots.

Soon after I yelled "cut," Reverend Run walked over to me and Jam Master Jay.

"Let me see the playback," he demanded.

"Let's get a couple of takes first, while the crowd is hot," I said in an attempt to delay showing him the wide take, "then I'll show you."

"I want to see it now!" Run demanded.

This was not going to be good. We played it back, and I knew he would not be happy. What I didn't know was how angry he would instantly get.

"He lied to me, Jam!" Run shouted in anger. "The director lied to me."

"No he didn't," Jam replied. "We gonna get it."

"The director lied to me."

"We are shooting you tight next," I said. He chose not to listen, ignoring me as if I wasn't even there.

"The director lied to me. Tell the director to shoot my face now."

I knew then that I had lost his trust for the rest of the night. He now had zero faith in me. He would not look at me or listen to anything I had to say, not even for a split second. He kept speaking to me through Jam Master Jay as I was standing beside them.

We captured seven takes, then proceeded to shoot the street scenes with Run-DMC and D-Generation X. Each time I had to explain what we were filing in a scene, I would have to communicate through my "translator," Jam.

"This motherfucker is going to love this video after we cut it," I said to myself.

When the shoot was over, Run-DMC became great friends with Triple H, Stephanie McMahon and the other members of D-Generation X. They hugged, laughed and exchanged handshakes as they said goodbye. Reverend Run? Not even a glance came my way.

The next day, I was in New York City overseeing the film-to-tape transfer. That's when we convert film into video and sync the audio to the tape so that we can edit the video. One hour into the session, I got a call from the receptionist.

"I'm calling for David."

"This is David."

"There is a Mister Run who just showed up and wants to join your session. Is that okay?"

"Yes. Send him up."

This was totally unexpected. I was completely caught off guard.

"Fast forward to the tight shots of Reverend Run singing," I told the editor with frenzy in my voice.

"Why?"

"Just trust me. We only have thirty seconds."

Run entered the edit room without knocking and took a seat beside me. He still would not make eye contact or talk to me. Instead, he spoke directly to the editor.

"Let me see the footage," he commanded. So we played it.

Twenty seconds in he grabbed my arm in a gentle way and turned to face me.

"This is fucking great!" he said with joy and wonder in his eyes. "This is fucking killer. I love it!"

"I'm glad you do," I responded.

"And you got tight shots of my face while I was singing!"

"I told you I would."

"Can I ask you a favor please, Mr. Director?"

"Of course you can."

"I want a bottle of white zinfandel. Can you make that happen?"

"Absolutely. Coming right up."

I called the receptionist and in less than ten minutes a chilled bottle of white zinfandel was delivered. He finished the entire bottle in thirty minutes.

"What is your name?" he asked.

"David. David Sahadi."

"Mr. David, can I ask another favor?"

"Yes, you can."

"I'd like another bottle of white zinfandel."

"Coming right up."

He grabbed my arm time and time again, in a gentle, familiar way. The video enthralled him, and he was beyond happy. He stayed for another hour before leaving.

"You did right by me," he said with a smile as he looked directly into my eyes. "Sorry if I was a bitch to you last night."

"You weren't," I replied, a lie concealed with a smile. "Everything came together and it's going to be a great music video when I am done cutting it. I promise you that."

"I believe you now. We never did anything like this before. Thank you."

And with those words he stood, extended his hand for a shake and left the edit room with a heart full of gratitude and relief.

But the story didn't end there. Two days later I sent the first edit to Run and his brother Russell Simmons, the co-owner of Def Jam Records. Within an hour I got a call on my cellphone from an unknown number.

"Is this David Sahadi?"

"Yes it is."

"This is Russell Simmons, and I just saw the video."

"Did you like it?"

"No! You have to get rid of all those lame-ass girls dancing on the streets. They are killing me brother, killing me bad."

"I just wanted to add a little sex appeal amid the violence."

"Bro, they killing me. Looks like 1980s shit. Everything is great except for the girls. Get rid of them."

And so I did. Just days before the music video would debut on MTV. To a worldwide, prime-time audience. To acclaimed critical success, despite all the unnecessary personal duress.

12

MY FAVORITE COMMERCIALS

Decrepit warehouses, neon lights, explosions and a great white shark. Sights, smells and sounds.

Those are some of the images and elements I would use in my commercials.

"What are your favorite spots you ever produced?" is a question I am often asked.

"There are so many" is always my reply, "way too many to classify as my favorites."

A dozen or so still bring me joy to this day. They are the commercials that presented the wrestlers as fish out of water in real-life settings, rather than in a wrestling ring.

Two that first come to mind featured The Rock promoting the WWF's video games. One was for *WrestleMania 2000*, and in the first shot we see him sitting in the back of a stretch limousine, apparently talking to his agent.

"Who's this Roody Poo Jabroni imitating me?" The Rock complains.

Another scene shows him in a hot tub with three beautiful models. Instead of flirting, he's complaining because the game's virtual character resembles him so closely.

"He walks like The Rock. He talks like The Rock."

We cut to shots of the video game, then to a scene of The Rock sitting in a diner. Now he complains to the waiter behind the counter.

"Heck, he even sounds like The Rock!" he says. "That's gimmick infringement."

As the camera pans to the waiter, we see it is an Elvis Presley impersonator, wiping a plate.

"That ain't right," the Elvis look-alike replies.

Then we cut back to a video screen in The Rock's limo as a cartoon character turns to him and commands, "Know your role and shut your mouth!"

The Rock then does his signature eyebrow raise in outrage.

For the ending, we cut back to an overhead shot of The Rock sitting on a toilet, his pants down to his ankles. In the stall beside him is Santa Claus.

"I want you to take all those video games in your green bag and shove them up your candy ass!" The Rock says. Santa then shoots him the bird.

"A brilliant concept was executed beautifully thanks to The Rock, Elvis and Santa," Ryan Dilbert of the Bleacher Report remarked. "How's that for an All-Star team? What some consider the best wrestling video game of all time doesn't stand up to the game of today, but this was as fun as this ad for it. And video game Rock talking smack to the real Rock is the highlight of a great spot."

The following year we filmed another video game commercial in South Beach, this one for *WWF: SmackDown 2*. This time The Rock is happy, recognized and exalted.

In the opening shot, we see the exterior of the hotel and The Rock walking through the fancy doors.

"Shine this up real nice, Jabroni," he tells the doorman upon entering the hotel, flipping a silver coin high into the air. The doorman catches it.

"And I know just where to stick it, Rock," the doorman happily exclaims as we see extras fighting outside in the background and Dr. Tom Prichard body-slamming D-Lo Brown, take after take, on the steel hood of a vintage car.

"What's your name?" The Rock asks the beautiful receptionist as she slides him the room key.

"It doesn't matter what my name is," she coyly replies in a soft, seductive voice.

The Rock then walks unexpectedly into the hotel's kitchen. "I can smell what you're cooking."

"Pancakes, Rock!" the head chef responds. "Pancakes!" Behind him stands Kane, calm as could be, as flames engulf the kitchen and utter mayhem unfolds around him.

At this point we cut to clips of the video game as the booming voice of the announcer is heard. Then we go back to The Rock, now relaxing at poolside with a tropical drink in his hand.

"Finally The Rock has come back to PlayStation," he declares as a well-dressed server beside him gets speared into the pool by Edge.

The spots I loved most, though, were the cross-channel ones we would produce for our monthly pay-per-view events. These spots did not air solely on WWF programming. They were sent to every cable system at the time, and they would air whenever the local station couldn't sell all of its advertising time, which was quite often. They would randomly appear on ESPN, A&E, CNN, Fox News, you name it. And I knew they weren't seen just by hardcore wrestling audiences but a larger mainstream audience instead.

"Know your audience" is what I often preached to my staff. Where is this spot airing? What is the demographic that will view this? What are their passions and desires? They were the people we could reach, the ones we could connect with.

In 1998, I had an epiphany. It was an overarching idea, yet so obvious and simple: Do not sell a spot that focuses on a wrestling match to an audience that couldn't give a damn about professional wrestling. Entertain them, make them laugh. So I went outside the box with these spots in an effort to amuse the non-wrestling audience. These viewers may not be fans of the WWF, but I wanted to make them fans of the commercials. Eventually, I hoped, the viewer would say, "Hey, I'm not a WWF fan, but I love all these WWF spots I have been seeing over the past few months. They are very funny. I might check out their show one day."

In most of the spots I produced after that, the viewer wouldn't even know it was a commercial for professional wrestling until at least halfway through. My goal was to hook them in the first few seconds so that they would continue watching whatever this commercial was promoting. Those first few seconds, those first impressions, were crucial. Quickly draw them in before they have time to reach for the remote and change the channel.

In one spot for the Royal Rumble, I did a spoof on the classic baseball movie *Field of Dreams*. That Academy Award–winning film featured a farmer, played by Kevin Costner, who hears the mystical message "if you build it, they will come." Costner proceeds to turn a patch of his large cornfield into a baseball field, and eventually the ghosts of famous baseball players from a bygone era emerge from the corn. Including the ghost of his father.

In this parody, we opened with a wide view of a cornfield before cutting to a tight shot of a farmer deep in its midst, who hears the same words: "If you build it, they will come." We then cut to multiple shots of the farmer tirelessly cutting down stalks of corn and hammering iron into the ground to build something. When he finishes, his wife appears carrying a tray with a large jug of iced tea and two glasses. As they smile, we cut to a crane shot that slowly rises to reveal what he'd been building — not a baseball field, but a WWF wrestling ring.

Suddenly we hear what sounds like the rolling thunder of bison charging over a small hill nearby. The couple's smiles vanish because instead of WWF superstars arriving, an army of Amish people — dressed in flannel blue shirts, black hats and black pants with suspenders — are racing over the hill toward the ring. Then we hear the feathering rustle of corn stalks opposite the Amish, and an equal number of "little people" emerge from the field. The Amish and the little people clash in the ring as an all-out brawl ensues.

"That's not what I had in mind," the disappointed farmer says to his wife. He wanted real wrestlers to appear. Instantly the spot cuts to a short sequence of graphics and highlights of WWF superstars.

"Thirty wrestlers," the announcer says. "One ring. Something's gotta give! The WWF presents the Royal Rumble, live on pay-per-view."

Then we cut back to the defeated Amish walking slowly, dejectedly, back up the hill from where they came.

"We'll get them little rascals next time," one Amish man says to another as the spot ends.

The following year, we did a sequel to the *Field of Dreams* parody for the Royal Rumble.

This time the spot takes place in an old western town from the late eighteenth century. A man is constructing a building and hears the iconic words "if you build it, they will come." He stops that work and begins building what is soon revealed as a WWF wrestling ring. The crane rises to show the ring on the town's main street, a dirt road with two-story wooden buildings along each side. The wide shot includes two saloons, a hotel, a barber shop and a bank. It looks like a scene from an old Clint Eastwood movie.

The thunderous rumble of a stampede is heard again. This time it's thirty sumo wrestlers turning the corner and racing to the ring. Across the street, the little people once again emerge, this time from the saloon. Again, the little people are victorious.

Another favorite spot I conceived was for the event "No Mercy," which would air in late October. That year the WWF was buying time during the MLB playoffs, and I knew the Yankees would play deep into the postseason. The commercial I wrote and directed was aimed at the baseball audience since it would be seen on various cable networks that didn't cater to the WWF. They would not know it was a wrestling spot until ten seconds in.

The commercial featured baseball players dressed in uniforms that looked nearly identical to the iconic pinstripes worn by the New York Yankees. As a bonus, I was able to commission John Sterling, the Yankees' equally iconic play-by-play announcer, to voice-over the spot for a mere $5,000.

The spot opens with tight shots of the pitcher intensely peering toward home plate followed by the hand of the catcher relaying the signs. Then the pitcher releases a mighty fastball, and we see it speeding toward home plate in a close-up shot created by CGI graphics. As all this is unfolding, we hear the play-by-play call of Sterling.

"Two outs. Bottom of the ninth. It all comes down to this for the Big Red Machine." (The Big Red Machine was also the nickname of baseball's Cincinnati Reds.)

Just then the camera reveals it is Kane in the batter's box, in full wrestling garb and his signature red mask. As the pitch reaches home plate, Kane unleashes a mighty swing, which we intercut with three different angles and synced with a thunderous sound effect that implied a monstrous home run. Flash cubes pop, and the crowd rises in awe.

"This could be it!" Sterling says.

But it's not a home run, merely a dribbler to the pitcher's mound. As the pitcher reaches for the ball to make an easy game-winning out, he gets speared by Edge. Then John Bradshaw clotheslines the first baseman, allowing Kane, now running the bases, to cruise past first. As Kane rounds second, the Hardy Boyz jump off ladders and take out the shortstop and second baseman. Kane then looks like he'll be out at third, but Faarooq nails the third baseman in the back with a garbage can just in time. Even the mascot tries to stop him from scoring but gets mauled by Kane himself.

Kane crosses the plate and it's a home run after all, aided by a few "errors," and it scores the winning run.

"The WWF wins, thaaaaaa WWF wins!" Sterling exclaims, a takeoff on his signature line whenever the Yankees won.

This is followed by "WWF: No Mercy" in a booming voice-over on the tag page, and the spot ends with the umpire scolding the wrestlers: "You're outta here!" the ump screams, just before Edge spears him.

"That's gotta hurt," Sterling comments.

An interesting footnote is that Frankie Kazarian, then an unknown to the nation, played the roles of the catcher and first and third baseman as well. Kazarian took the brutal garbage can shot to the back, not once but nine times.

After the third take, I knew we had the shot.

"Give me one more take," Faarooq pleaded. "I can do better."

I obliged. Six more times, actually, before I realized he was playing me and just wanted to brutalize Kazarian. When I finally said that's enough, Faarooq laughed heartily. To Frankie's credit, he knew what was going on well before I did, but he never once complained.

As Frankie recalls it:

> There's a scene where I field a ball at third base and Ron Simmons comes up behind me and hits me with the trash can. We must've done the scene about nine times.
>
> I only found out years later that we had the take in the first or second shot. Apparently, Ron just wanted to rib me and teach me a bit. Honestly, it didn't bother me one bit.

> At that time I would do whatever it takes to get myself to the next level. I loved every second of it.
>
> Filming the No Mercy baseball commercial was at the time for me such a thrill and a highlight. I was getting to work with WWE superstars, and a WWE director, David Sahadi. I love baseball and it is my favorite sport, so that also helped. We shot all night long and I was used in multiple spots.

Speaking of Kane, he was also featured in the commercial for "No Mercy" one year later. It was a spot that featured the legendary and controversial baseball player Pete Rose. Halloween was the theme, and it featured a bunch of young trick-or-treaters dressed as WWE superstars and knocking on Rose's door. One was dressed as Kurt Angle, another as Hulk Hogan, and other kids as Chris Jericho, Stone Cold Steve Austin, The Undertaker and The Rock.

Every time Rose opens his door he looks disgusted as the kids deliver each wrestler's unique catchphrase. Rose verbally berates the trick-or-treaters and slams the door on them.

"Candy for an Olympic hero?" asks the first youngster, dressed like Angle.

"No candy for you. It's true, it's true," replies Rose, throwing Angle's catchphrase back at the kid.

"Trick or treat, brother," says the one in the Hogan costume.

"Get lost," Rose replies, slamming the door shut. And so on.

Eventually there's a louder knock on the door. As Rose opens it, his disgust turns to horror. Standing there, just two feet away, is Kane.

"Hello Pete," says Kane, who then grabs Rose by the throat and bodyslams him onto the wooden planks of the front porch.

This spot was the culmination of a two-year storyline that saw Rose tease and torment wrestling fans time and time again before Kane would appear and give him a tombstone piledriver. One year Rose even dressed up disguised as the San Diego Chicken mascot and fiendishly attacked Kane from behind, but to no avail.

While these spots were designed for a non-wrestling audience, they were beloved by WWF fans. My goal was to produce a commercial that entertained the viewer and gave them a lasting, positive impression about our product.

Another one of my all-time favorites was the last spot I would ever shoot for WWE (as it had been rebranded by then). It was a takeoff on an iconic scene from the movie *Jaws*.

The commercial opens with a wide shot of a calm beach on an idyllic summer afternoon, with the sounds of seagulls flying above and the laughter of children playing in the sand. Then a lifeguard slowly rises from his high perch and starts blowing his whistle to alarm the beachgoers. A young, bikini-clad girl gets up from a beach blanket and suddenly witnesses something in the sea before her.

"*Shark!*" she screams.

Then we cut to a shot of the police sheriff with the "Spielberg effect" — a special lens-and-dolly combination where the dolly pulls away at the same time the lens is zooming in tighter. (Spielberg used the technique in a similar scene in *Jaws*.) This effect gave the viewer an impression of surrealness and captured the concern on the sheriff's face, illustrating that his deepest fears were being realized.

"Everybody out of the water!" the police chief commands, panic in his voice. "Get out of the water now!"

Beachgoers frantically run away from the surf, and in the chaos we catch a quick blur of a muscular person in black tights and wrestling boots running with purpose the opposite way, toward the ocean. It's Brock Lesnar!

Lesnar dives headfirst into a wave. When he resurfaces, a great white shark is right on his shoulders. He gives the shark a mighty F5 slam into the surf (which we shot and cut with many different camera angles). Lesnar emerges the fearless hero.

We only filmed one take of Lesnar's dive into the oncoming wave. He apparently mistimed it and dove when the wave was half its original size. Brock told me he felt a little woozy and possibly had a slight concussion, so I would not allow him to do another take. Anyone who knows the dangers of concussions, whether in pro wrestling or the NFL, would understand.

Over time, as I produced these funny, entertaining and image-driven spots on a regular, monthly basis, our audience grew.

I knew it would.

13

MY FAVORITE WWE SUPERSTARS

Pyrotechnics with huge fireballs and explosions. The vividly colored neon streets of South Beach, Florida. Dark, abandoned warehouses with vicious dogs, saliva dripping from their mouths.

I always tried to find a location with the atmosphere and imagery that would truly enhance the character of the wrestler I was working with. Every shoot for each individual talent was unique for them.

There were many wrestlers I loved to work with. They knew the dramatic images I filmed in these locations would make them look like superheroes and elevate their personas.

Stone Cold Steve Austin was one of my favorites to work with. His character proclaimed "don't trust anyone," but Steve always trusted the production team at the WWF.

Every shoot I did with Austin portrayed him as an intrepid warrior walking through streets set ablaze and giant fireballs exploding around him. Sometimes he'd even walk through these twelve-foot-high fireballs of propane mixed with gasoline. Nothing could deter or distract him; this rugged warrior was fearless, walking through the chaos of overturned, burning cars and people frantically running for their lives in every direction. And he remained stone cold. Steve Austin came across as menacing and invincible. Nothing could deter his mission, whatever it was.

The very first shoot I did with Austin was filmed on a miniscule budget in an abandoned warehouse on a damp night in late October 1996. No pyro. No huge fireballs. Just Austin at his rawest.

He had recently won the King of the Ring tournament, defeating Jake "The Snake" Roberts. Minutes later, as he was crowned king, he cut a legendary promo.

"Jake 'The Snake,'" Austin began, "you can quote John 3:16 and all the psalms of the bible. But Austin 3:16 says I just whooped your ass!"

The crowd erupted with applause. That signature line would propel him to cult hero status and sell millions of T-shirts. A star was born.

For Austin's next big match, against Bret "The Hitman" Hart in the "Survivor Series," our intent was to shoot four to five vignettes to air during *Monday Night Raw* to hype the event. My co-producer for the shoot was Chris Chambers, a great, creative visionary. We both knew the magnitude of these vignettes, and the location we found in Bridgeport, Connecticut, was a dreary set with piles of crumbled bricks and steel beams lying everywhere, devoid of anything that was comfortable.

We made one major mistake, however.

Neither Chris nor I wrote any scripts for Austin. Why would we? After the promo he cut about The Snake we thought that Stone Cold was a maestro with the microphone. We just wanted to let the cameras roll and have Austin freestyle, saying anything that came to his mind.

Oh, how wrong we were. On this night he was nothing like a maestro. As soon as he started speaking we realized the shoot had the potential to be a total disaster.

For fifteen minutes Austin rambled on and on, using run-on sentences that never made a strong point, never enhanced his character. He just kept spewing words that were not only simplistic but brought the image of the rising star crashing down to Earth, as if he was a mere mid-card wrestler. His thoughts were discombobulated, disconnected and lacked depth.

That one mistake, however, ended up being a blessing in the end.

"Steve, give us a few moments," I said as Chambers pulled me aside.

"This is horrible," he said.

"I know. What do you suggest?"

"Let's write a bunch of one-liners and have him deliver each of them one at a time."

"Great idea."

For another fifteen minutes that's what we did. On the dirty floor of this dark, decrepit warehouse, on scraps of wrinkled paper, Chambers and I wrote line after line before we resumed filming. I would feed Austin the lines one at a time.

"Steve," I said to him, "let's try something different."

"Okay. What do you have in mind?"

"I'm going to feed you a bunch of one-liners Chris and I just wrote, and we want you to read each one three times in a row with a different inflection each time."

"Sounds all right by me." Magic was about to unfold.

"Say 'Bret Hart' three times." And so he did, and we kept feeding him lines.

"Pink tights. Pink tights? Pink tights!"

"What the hell is that all about, Bret?"

"This ain't no ballet class."

"Sunglasses and sparklers."

"What a load of crap."

Those were just a few. They were short and to the point. In post-production, we used the lines over black-and-white shots of Austin pacing in the warehouse. We intercut those with tight shots of his face staring directly into the camera, making him look fierce and menacing. Sometimes we heard just his voice as he stared with purpose into the camera without moving his lips. Other times we actually saw him speak the words. We also intercut stock footage of rabidly barking dogs to put emphasis on a few of his lines. As we cut to the tag page, the musical genius Jim Johnston introduced the iconic sound of glass breaking that would precede Austin's entrance theme from that point on.

Days later, when Austin first viewed those vignettes, he was awestruck.

"Wow, that's incredible!" he exclaimed. "I love the black-and-white shots. And those barking dogs are great! I don't even remember seeing those dogs there!"

That's because they never were there. We added the shots of the dogs in post.

The match between Bret Hart and Steve Austin a month later was a classic. One of the things that Hart and Austin focused on was stipulating that the match would be submissions-only. This was interesting as Austin virtually never used submissions in the ring.

The match was beyond brutal. It began with a brawl, both competitors going in and out of the ring to break the ten-count. A number of weapons were also used. Eventually, Austin was busted open by Hart, but he never gave up. It was a gutsy performance of fortitude and endurance. Austin never looked weak, despite the fact he had no submission moves in his arsenal. Hart never looked out of his element either and adapted to Austin's brawling style.

At the end of the night, Hart put Austin into the sharpshooter. That was Hart's submission move and, once fully locked in, no one ever escaped from it. Austin, with blood pouring down his face, never submitted, never tapped out. Instead he "passed out" in a pool of his own blood in the center of the ring. When the final bell rang, Hart had suddenly become the heel; fans booed him throughout the arena. Austin had now become the face, and the ravenous crowed boisterously applauded him. A star was now shining at its brightest.

Triple H

Who would have thought the son-in-law of Vince McMahon, a WWE champion with privilege and entitlement, would make this list?

Most wouldn't. Triple H, however, is the rare exception.

When we worked together, Paul Levesque was human, not a megalomaniac. He truly cared. He sought advice and gave it in gentle, respectful ways. I felt blessed whenever I worked with him. He always cooperated, went above and beyond, and made me feel as important as he was.

Like the others at the top of my list, Triple H never complained on any shoot we did. Never. Not even when we filmed "The Cerebral Assassin" with him shirtless in an abandoned warehouse on a frigid December night when the temperature was way below freezing.

He was also a great, calming asset on shoots, too, especially in the stress created by Reverend Run during the filming of the Run-DMC music video. In the tension of that night, Triple H made Run feel at ease.

He gave him comfort, especially during the filming of the violent scenes on the streets. And on all shoots he would gently make suggestions, most of which I appreciated. That humbleness, that "willing to do anything" attitude on set proved he deeply cared.

On a personal level, there was one funny moment that happened in the locker room of WWE's elaborate gym at Titan Towers in 2002. It was the Friday before Triple H's main event title match against Hulk Hogan. As I was getting into my workout gear, Triple H emerged from the shower with a white towel wrapped around his waist.

"Hello David," he said.

"Hi Hunter," I replied. "I have a question for you."

"Shoot."

"So, is Hulk going to go over on Sunday?"

"No. Hulk is kind of like a Kiss reunion tour. It's great at first, but it gets old after a while, like a carton of milk."

Either Triple H had no idea about the eventual outcome or he was keeping it a secret from me. But why would he? He always told me everything whenever I asked because he knew the promos and ads I was producing for future events required me to know the storylines. He trusted me, so I believe to this day that what he said at that moment was what he truly believed. That's not what happened, though.

A month earlier, Triple H walked out of WrestleMania X8 as the undisputed champion, and for once he was a beloved babyface. Meanwhile, Hogan was coming off a dream match against The Rock, and despite a long absence, Hogan was so popular with the fans that even The Rock was booed during the match at WrestleMania.

"So I don't have to change any of the promos for the upcoming events?" I asked.

"No, you don't," he said. "I'll still be the champion."

The upcoming battle between Triple H and Hogan was at "Backlash," just one month after WrestleMania. The match was predictable, but in the end chaos broke loose as many WWE superstars stormed the ring. In the melee, Triple H was "knocked unconscious" with a chair shot to the head. Sensing opportunity, Hogan hit the leg drop, covered the champion and won the match. At age forty-nine, Hulk Hogan was once again the WWE world champion.

Triple H was either convinced to drop the belt to Hogan that night for a "feel good" moment for the fans, or he was working me. And in all honesty, I don't think he lied.

The Undertaker

"What do you need?" I'd always ask.

"Nothing," he'd always reply.

That's why my favorite of all time was and remains The Undertaker. Hands down. The fact that the shoots required huge fireballs and pyrotechnics was an added bonus.

Every shoot with "The Deadman" was from dusk to dawn, first in graveyards and then mostly in cold, abandoned warehouses. Why? Fire and flames look the best in the darkness of night. The Deadman knew that, and also knew these images would present him as the most dominating, otherworldly force on the planet.

"Hello Mark," I would say a week before each shoot just to give him a heads-up.

"Hello David," he'd reply.

"You are aware that we have a shoot next week in Connecticut?"

"Yes, I am aware," he would say. "Sundown to sunrise, correct?"

"Correct. As always."

"I'm cool with that."

"We will have a trailer for you to hang out in between takes and just relax. We also have a production assistant just for you to get you any food, water or anything else you may want."

"David, all I need is a case of Coors Light and a bottle of Jack Daniel's."

"That's it?"

"That's it."

That simple.

The Undertaker was always on time, and like the great ones that "get it," he never once complained. We would do dozens of takes each night, and after each one he'd ask, "How does it look?"

"It looks phenomenal! Come over here and I'll show you on the playback monitor." He was always pleased.

"When do you need me next?" he'd then say.

"In about twenty minutes, after we relight the set, reload the pyro and change camera angles."

"Just have someone knock on my trailer one minute beforehand."

"Sure thing." We would always give him that one-minute warning, and sure enough he was always on time.

The joy of working with one of the biggest superstars in the history of the business, creating iconic, brilliant images with pyro, smoke and fire, and never hearing a single complaint, is priceless.

So, too, was every opportunity to work with The Undertaker.

Kurt Angle

"It's true. It's true!" was Kurt Angle's very first catchphrase.

Yes, it is true: Angle, the Olympic gold medalist and world champion, is one of my favorite wrestlers to work with.

Whenever I worked with him, his attitude was always Olympian. Total pro. Never late. Never once complaining. Just like The Undertaker.

Angle battled many serious injuries throughout his career, including to his lower back and neck. Whenever we filmed Angle for a commercial or just for imagery shots, he would take several minutes to stretch and warm up. On every one of these shoots, I would silently motion my camera operator to roll the camera for a minute or two as he stretched, without Angle knowing we were actually filming. The motions he did, the grimaces of pain etched on his face, were painfully real. You could feel his physical torment through the screen when these moments were shot in slow motion. We would use these images in opening videos for our pay-per-view events as well as video packages and promos. If I asked Angle to stretch and pretend he was in pain, it would never come across as genuine. Acting can never capture a real moment.

Angle was featured in many commercial spots for WWE as well, including one for the *WWF: SmackDown 2* video game.

"The memories I had were being blown away at the way the spots we did came across on TV," Angle would say. "You knew it was something incredible."

One of my favorite shoots with Angle would come years later when I was working for TNA Wrestling. It, too, was a commercial for a video game.

The concept was devised and produced by an ad agency, but I was there as the creative director and advisor for TNA, so my input on set was greatly appreciated. The spot was shot in Los Angeles and the setting was a video game store.

"TNA has a video game?" a teenager asks his friend.

"Yes, and it's badass."

Suddenly, A.J. Styles jumps through the store's front window in full wrestling gear, glass shattering all around. Then Angle appears, toppling a large rack filled with video games that scatter all over the floor. The adversaries look at each other with aggressive intent and, as Angle roars, they charge. At the precise moment when they meet and simultaneously exchange a punch to the face, we cut to the exact same punch from the video game. Reality became animation in perfect synchronicity. The visuals were epic.

"The video game shoot was badass," Kurt said. "It made A.J. and I look like warriors. That's the magic of David Sahadi."

Well, it was only partly my magic. The real credit for this shoot goes to the ad agency, but I'll take Kurt's compliments.

Here's a funny side note. Before we began shooting this commercial on a sunny morning, Kurt was sitting outside getting some rays and reading a newspaper with the straps of his wrestling singlet lowered.

"Hey Joe," he said as I approached.

"What's up, Kurt?" I replied.

"Joe, do you like baseball?"

I was astonished. This was the second time in a row that he'd called me Joe. He always called me by my last name, Sahadi.

"Yes, I do."

"Who's your favorite team, Joe?"

"Kurt, my favorite team is the Yankees, and my name is David, not Joe."

He was completely sober and clear as could be, sipping coffee as he read the newspaper. It was just an innocent gaffe, one which he immediately acknowledged.

"I'm so sorry. I never call you David. I always say Sahadi."

I laughed. "Everyone calls me Sahadi. But I really do have a brother named Joe, though."

He laughed, too.

What I loved most about Kurt Angle was the respect, the warmth, and the gentleness that he always showed me whenever we worked together. Despite his Olympic gold medal and being a multi-time world champion, Angle always treated me like a brother and trusted friend. It was real. "Damn real," as Kurt would say.

And he never called me Joe again.

The friendship and bond that Angle and I formed at TNA lasts to this day.

Classy Freddie Blassie

Although he was not an active wrestler at the time, I would be remiss if I didn't include the Hall of Fame legend Classy Freddie Blassie. We first met while shooting a commercial for the "Raw Bowl," a Monday night episode of *Raw* that happened to fall on New Year's Eve. Professional wrestling has no off weeks. It is always a new episode, fifty-two weeks a year.

In this commercial, Blassie played the role of a football coach. He was standing at a platform trying to motivate his team in an emotional pregame speech by citing famous quotes from legendary coaches. His team was all WWF wrestlers — Owen Hart, Yokozuna and the British Bulldog, to name a few.

"What the hell are you doing here you old bastard?" I'd jokingly say upon his arrival whenever I saw him.

"Shut the hell up, you no-good piece of shit," he'd always reply. It was our way of saying, "I love you my good friend." Often, onlookers would think we were serious. One would have to understand the friendship Blassie and I shared to realize were just playing with each other.

I also featured Blassie in numerous cold opens for pay-per-view events. I called these "Freddie Fellini," as they were shot in the style of the great Federico Fellini, a famous Italian director in the 1930s, as an homage. We filmed them in black and white and color-corrected the wrestling footage to black and white as well. There was no voice-over or sound bites. The emotion was conveyed through classic dramatic music and the odd characters that would pop in around Blassie from time to time.

I filmed many commercial spots with the living legend as the lead, including a four-part series for Laser Jet as well as the annual holiday spot. In a spot that could never be aired today, we decorated the main lobby of Titan Towers to look like a typical department store. Blassie was dressed as Santa, sitting in front of a Christmas tree. And boy, was he as dirty as ever.

"Get a look at those," he exclaims at one point as a girl walks past him in disgust.

"Hey lady," he says to another fine-looking woman, "how'd you like to sit on Santa's knees and talk about whatever comes up?" Horrified, she also walks away.

Then the elevator doors open and out walks one of the most beautiful models I ever hired. Freddie takes notice and starts to lower his beard before speaking.

"Hey Toots, how'd you like to wake up Christmas morning and find me lying naked underneath your Christmas tree?"

Unlike the women who took offense, this model looks at Freddie, raises an eyebrow and smiles. As we cut to black, the voice of Blassie is heard in the background.

"Ho ho ho! Santa's gonna get some tonight!"

Besides on-air spots, I also used Blassie's deep and raspy voice for the narration of a dozen or so other opening videos.

Sadly, we lost Freddie Blassie on June 2, 2003. That was my final month at WWE before I took a sabbatical. Freddie never knew.

I arrived at the hospital the day before he passed. His wife, Miyako, who had been by his side for several days and nights, told me that his eyes hadn't opened for days.

After twenty solemn minutes, I approached my dear friend Freddie and kissed his forehead. Then I leaned in, gave him a hug and whispered in his right ear.

"You can go now, Freddie," I gently said. "It's okay. We will all be okay. Go now if you wish, my friend. Know that we will always love you and you will live forever in our hearts."

Then I heard Miyako scream.

"*Look!* His eyes! They are open!"

I stepped back and looked at Freddie. His eyes were indeed wide open, staring up at the ceiling and perhaps at what lay beyond. I rushed out of the room and into the hall to release a torrent of tears. I didn't want Freddie to see them, not now, not in this moment of anguish.

"Why did you run out?" a friend of the family asked as he approached me in the hall while I was sitting on the tile floor.

"Look," I said as I turned my head to face him. He saw how hard I'd been crying. "I cannot let Freddie see me like this. He will feel my sadness."

"You really do love him, don't you?"

"More than anyone will ever know."

The Rock

For nearly a decade, The Rock was also one of my favorite stars to work with. We had known each other since he'd first started training to become a wrestler at our Stamford warehouse. We formed an instant bond.

We filmed spots in Los Angeles and South Beach, making him look like a Hollywood star before he became one. We shot in diners, limousines and fancy nightclubs and included all the things famous stars have access to.

It was always a joy to work with The Rock. That is, until he had one bad night in the spring of 2003 . . .

14

THE ROCK

There are so many great things one can say about The Rock, both as a WWE superstar and a king of Hollywood.

And a really bad one as well.

When I first met Dwayne Johnson, he was training in the bowels of the WWE studios. His teacher was the great Dr. Tom Prichard. Johnson was an unknown then.

"You are going to be a superstar one day!" were the first words I spoke to him.

"Why do you say that?" he asked.

"You have a million-dollar smile. A great attitude. And I can feel your charisma. It oozes out of every pore of your being."

"Thanks," he replied. "You made my day."

We would chat a few times a week back while he was training, when the wrestling world had no idea who he would become, the phenomenon he would create. Once in a while I'd even treat him to dinner at a local restaurant, the Black Goose in Darien, Connecticut, just a stone's throw away from Stamford. He was an ambitious kid then, busting his ass training every day. I just wanted to validate his dreams and give him a small dose of hope.

When he finally made his in-ring debut for the WWF in the fall of 1996, he was introduced as Rocky Maivia, a combination of his father and grandfather's ring names (they were both wrestlers). He was also nicknamed the "Blue Chipper," and to play up his lineage he was hyped as the WWF's first third-generation wrestler. Rocky was heavily pushed as a clean-cut babyface despite his lack of wrestling experience. And within three months he became the WWF Intercontinental Champion when he defeated Hunter Hearst Helmsley, Triple H, in February 1997.

But the fans would have none of it. Despite his being a babyface and saying all the right things, the crowd felt he was pushed too fast. Wrestling fans are a savvy bunch, and they booed him heavily. Soon the fans would serenade him with chants of "die Rocky die" and "Rocky sucks" during his matches. Two months later he dropped the title to Owen Hart, and early that summer he suffered a serious knee injury while wrestling Mankind. He spent several months off-air while recovering.

When he returned to television, Rocky was a secondary player in a new faction, the "Nation of Domination." His character was an angry heel then, especially toward the fans who booed him as a babyface, and he would often insult and chide the crowd. It was both a "work" and a "shoot." Deep down he really was upset that the fans wouldn't cheer for him when he was just the good guy.

Several weeks later while standing behind Faarooq, the leader of the Nation of Domination, during an in-ring promo, The Rock raised an eyebrow. It wasn't planned or deliberate, but it was a magical moment, a spark we all saw in real time. It was subtle, yet it was a seismic change that would lead to the making of a legend.

The first time I worked with The Rock was in an abandoned warehouse with a few new superstars we wanted to feature in an updated version of the original Attitude spot. He wasn't a big star yet, but we knew he was about to break out.

When that day came, Chris Chambers and I helped persuade Johnson to refer to himself in the third person as "The Rock" whenever he cut a promo. I am not sure if that idea came from Chambers or someone else on the creative team, but we constantly encouraged him to do it.

"Why?" he would ask.

"Because you will be a hated heel if you refer to yourself in the third person."

It took a couple of months for him to fully embrace and become that character. Initially, he would mix "I" and "The Rock" in the same sentence, but soon he would nail it.

"So The Rock was backstage . . ."

"The Rock thinks . . ."

"The Rock is going to lay a smackdown on your candy ass!"

I worked with The Rock nearly a dozen times in the years that followed. Some of my favorite commercials featured him, such as spots for the *WrestleMania 2000* and *WWF: SmackDown 2* video games. Much of the imagery for the pay-per-view commercials featured shoots with The Rock as well. I even directed the music video of The Rock that was sung by Method Man and was one of the top songs on the *Aggression* album. He never complained once when we shot the video in South Beach. He knew the way he was being directed would enhance his image.

Most of what I did with The Rock over the years was shot in and around Miami. I tried to make it easy for him, since he lived roughly twenty-five miles away in Davie, Florida. My dad was often an extra in those shoots, and they formed a bond. Poppa Lou really loved The Rock. The respect was mutual.

I would always call The Rock directly to inform him of the dates and times of the shoots and what was required. This was never a problem . . . until he went to Hollywood. Then everything changed.

Ever since I arrived at the WWF, we would do at least one "ID" shoot with all of the talent on the roster each year. These shoots all required a unique, visually intriguing set and were often shot in abandoned warehouses in Connecticut, New York or Los Angeles. We would supplement the cool imagery of the unique locations with a bevy of special effects such as rain machines, lightning strikes or pyrotechnics.

We would capture images of the talent with wide and tight shots, especially their faces and individual signature poses. Obviously I would allot more time on set for the top superstars, and just five minutes or so for those lower on the roster. The images we captured would be used in promos, packages, video walls and digital media.

In the spring of 2003, I decided to do an ID shoot in Miami. The Rock was returning from Hollywood after finishing his latest movie and was booked for the main event against Brock Lesnar in a major upcoming pay-per-view. So I decided to build the set backstage at the American Airlines arena, just thirty minutes from his home in Davie. He was back home and wanted to work a house match in Miami to get the rust off and get back into wrestling shape. By this time, I could no longer call The Rock personally. I had to go through both his agent and publicist first.

On this shoot, I discovered the man I once knew and respected had changed. Nine months earlier, he'd left WWE to shoot another Hollywood movie. I sent him three books upon his return to the world of celluloid heroes — books I thought would resonate with him, words I thought would speak to his spirit because they spoke to mine. The books were *Illusions* by Richard Bach, *The Alchemist* by Paulo Coelho, and *The Prophet*, penned by Kahlil Gibran nearly a century ago.

I greeted The Rock when he arrived at the arena for the ID shoot.

"Hey Rock," I said. "As you know, we brought the set here to make it easy on you."

"I know," he replied. "Thank you for that."

"I can shoot you whenever you wish. It'll only take twenty or twenty-five minutes."

"Give me an hour to settle in. I want to say hello to the boys first."

"Okay."

I didn't give him an hour. I gave him two. Then I searched for him backstage. He was playing cards with a group of wrestlers and agents.

"Is now a good time for you, Rock?" He was still in his street clothes, two hours after his arrival.

"Let me finish this game first."

Another hour passed, so I sought him out again. He was finally starting to put on his wrestling gear.

"Looks like you are getting ready for the shoot," I remarked.

"Yes."

Yet another hour passed. Now he was in full gear, but he was talking to his opponent.

"Are you ready to go now?" I asked. "It'll be fast."

"No. I need to go over the match first. Then I'll come to you."

I was not happy.

"I need you. We came here for you," I said in a stern voice.

"I know. I'll find you when we are done planning the match. I promise."

He never found me. Instead I found him an hour later backstage near the Gorilla Position, a secret control area that is always close to the entrance to the arena. He was watching a match on one of the many screens there.

"Now?" I asked, a tinge of hope mixing with a healthy dose of anger in my voice.

"Not now. After my match."

By this point I was fuming. I'd gone out of my way to make this shoot as painless as possible for him, yet I felt he was going out of *his* way to ignore and neglect me. And WWE as a whole.

As his entrance theme played, he walked through the black curtain that separates secrets from fantasy and into the deafening roar of a thunderous crowd. During the match I waited, steadfast, on the other side of the black curtain. When his match was finally over he walked backstage, and I made sure I was the first person he would see.

He was sweating profusely, and when he saw me waiting he wasn't happy.

"Rock," I said in a voice that left no doubt I was angry. "Now, right here." I pointed to the set fifteen feet away.

"Really, D?" he replied with fury. "Really?"

"Yes. Really. We came here just for you and you've been blowing me off all day."

He huffed heavily and got even angrier. "You get five minutes," he commanded, holding five fingers in front of my face. "Five minutes. That's all."

"I'll take it."

One minute into the shoot I heard a sound I knew and always dreaded. It was the sound of a hair stuck in the gate of the camera lens. Why was this happening now?

"What's that?" Rock snapped.

"We just have to check the gate."

"How long is that going to take?"

"Just a few minutes."

He was pissed. He was ready to walk off the set.

But as angry as he was, I was even more furious. Such disregard, I thought, after all I had done for him and all the sacrifices we'd made collectively to help jump-start his career. Still, I tried to ease the tension.

"Rock, did you get the three books I sent you?"

That question took him by surprise. I knew it would. Now I was playing him.

"What books?"

"The ones I said I would send to you in Los Angeles nine months ago. Remember? It was the last time we worked together."

"I never got them."

"Funny," I remarked. "I got the receipt from FedEx and I saw your signature and the date you received them."

His attitude changed drastically. His snarky smirk turned into that famous million-dollar smile, and his demeanor became calm and friendly, fake as it was. He was trying to play me now.

"How's your father doing?" he asked, gently putting his hand on my shoulder. Damn, he is a great actor, I thought, but he was desperate for redemption.

As Heath Ledger said while playing the character of the Joker, "Sometimes you have to play the role of a fool to fool the fool who thinks he is fooling you." So I played the role, and The Rock couldn't fool me now.

"He's doing great," I replied with a smile. Now I had the power, the control, over this king of Hollywood.

"Why isn't he here tonight, D?"

"He had something better to do."

"Tell him I say hello. Will you please?"

"I certainly will," I replied, but I would not.

A minute later the camera was ready, and he now allowed us to roll for not five but fifteen minutes. When we were finished, he shook my hand and said thanks. It mattered little. It was all a falsehood. He revealed a side to me I never thought he had, one I never wanted to see.

Everyone is allowed to have a bad day in life. I've had many. We all have. The Rock just happened to have a really bad one that day, so I will give him a pass.

It's just sad that it was the last time I would ever work with him.

15

VINCE MCMAHON

Reprehensible. Charming. Ruthless. Charismatic. Loved. Loathed.

All of those words could be used to describe the devil.

Or Vince McMahon.

People say a lot of horrible things about McMahon. He's been accused of many despicable acts that people are eager to speak about, to either call him out or tear him down. Yet he is human, and although he might have done some appalling things, he has also uplifted and taken care of a lot of people, too.

I was blessed because I was one of them.

Although I heard many dark stories of his mischievous behaviors, I never saw them in person. I'm not denying that they happened — all I know is that when I was in his presence he was always respectful and gracious, and treated me like a son. So I cannot judge Vince McMahon by what others say. I judge Vince solely by the way he treated me.

Of the myriad things that encapsulate his legacy, no one can dispute the fact that Vince was an astute businessman, a visionary, and a pioneer who crossed lines and ruthlessly destroyed many territories in his quest to create an empire. And an empire is what he created.

As I said earlier, what Vince told me in his private office on my first day of work — "It's all about emotion" — has stuck with me ever since. Those words echo through eternity, forever in my heart.

Some people are saddled by emotion. I am a person with many. Elation, sadness, depression and hope. I acknowledge these emotions and feel them deeply, but do not become tethered to them. Instead I control them and channel them into everything I do. They are fuel to my creativity. I fully tap into and embrace whatever emotion I am feeling to conceive and produce a stunning cold open for a major pay-per-view event, or channel it to imagine, invent and produce an ambitious ad campaign. Or write a poem!

McMahon had a very creative mind, but there were times when we collectively had to protect him from bad ideas.

One example was when Stone Cold Steve Austin's star was still ascending, and Vince was unhappy. McMahon wanted Austin to be a heel that the fans hated, not cheered. It ate at him.

In his epic match with Bret "The Hitman" Hart, which stipulated the loser would have to tap out, Stone Cold did not. Instead he "bled out" in a pool of his own blood. The bell rang, and Hart won the match — but Austin won the crowd.

Vince hastily arranged a meeting in the boardroom of Titan Towers. Present were the top people in TV production as well as a few executives in Vince's inner circle.

"I want people to boo Steve Austin," McMahon told everyone in frustration. "Instead, they are cheering him. We need a strong heel right now, and the fans are making him a babyface."

A stunned silence filled the room. A few moments later, McMahon continued.

"Maybe we should turn him back into the ringmaster-type character. Let his blond hair turn back to stubble. And maybe we have him wear those baby-blue tights again. Thoughts?"

We all had thoughts, and none were aligned with McMahon's. For a minute or two no one spoke. My thought was, why the fuck would we stop this rocket from ascending? Finally, Kevin Dunn spoke.

"Vince, the crowd is loving this character. Let's just go with it and see where it takes us. You always preached 'listen to the crowd,' and the crowd is now speaking."

Vince acquiesced. The Stone Cold Steve Austin phenomenon would soon emerge, and he would become one of the most transcendental characters in the history of professional wrestling.

Vince had many bad ideas. Some we could not talk him out of, such as the fake Razor Ramon and Diesel characters mentioned earlier. Another was the infamous "Katie Vick" vignette, where Triple H faked having necrophiliac sex with a corpse in a casket. Vince also turned the fledgling XFL into a trashy version of professional wrestling three weeks in as the football league was faltering in the ratings.

In sum, Vince McMahon is a conundrum, a paradox — brilliant and bold, despicable and degenerate. He had many demons, and his biggest flaw was that he couldn't exorcize them all because they were buried so deep inside.

Yet I solely judge him by the way he treated me. Respectful, loving, warm and smiling. Always smiling. And I fondly remember the many pats on the back that were always accompanied by "thanks pal!"

I was one of the lucky few that Vince showed that elusive, tiny, shiny sliver of the good side of his heart. If only this visionary could be that way with everyone.

Vince McMahon respected the hell out of me . . . until the day he found out I was about to leave WWE.

16

TIME TO LEAVE

With great success eventually comes great excess.

Excess of riches, of new employees commanding huge salaries, of a lot of things that are unnecessary.

That's what happened when WWE went public in October of 2000. Suddenly there was an excess of new hires, high-level executives from other networks who thought they knew better than us — me and all those creative, talented people who'd never lost hope, who endured the tough times with heart and passion solely because they'd embraced the vision that would eventually create this mighty empire.

The new hires thought *they* were the experts. In actuality they were mostly cast-offs from other networks with bloated resumes. There is a reason one redesigns their resume: They need a job. Their carefully worded bios were the best things they ever brought to the best company they would ever work for.

Out of nowhere I suddenly had several levels I needed to go through to bring my visions to fruition, and several other layers to speak directly with Vince McMahon. The discards were power-hungry, and in their eyes we were mere "wrestling guys."

All of my outside-the-box ideas, which had helped make WWE what it was, became sanitized. The new people in charge wanted me to do things their way, and their way was boring, clichéd and outdated, a throwback to a decade earlier. That was the era they'd once ruled but didn't want to evolve from. They were stuck in a loop they did not want to escape from, however outdated their ideas were.

I slowly became disenchanted. The fun of working there was fading. Instead of a creative atmosphere, the corporate world had taken over, like a dark cloud blocking the sun.

One thing I found egregious was an idea, or should I say ultimatum, from a new executive, Bonnie Werth. She wanted me to tag every thirty-second spot I produced for a monthly pay-per-view event with a "value-added item." For instance, "Order WWE Backlash and receive a free Undertaker bandanna with proof of purchase." I was against it for many reasons. I felt it cheapened us.

I finally blew a gasket when I was instructed to include a value-added item in a spot for WrestleMania. Really?

Just for insight, a thirty-second spot consisted of twenty-three seconds of trying to stir the viewer's emotions, then a seven-second tag page. Tacking on a value-added tag page with voice-over took another nine seconds, which left me only fourteen seconds to promote the event and provoke emotion. Preposterous.

"I am not adding that to the spot for WrestleMania," I defiantly said.

"Yes you are," she commanded.

"WrestleMania, in name only, sells itself. It does not need a 'value-added' item to get fans to purchase it. If anything, it cheapens us."

"Tell me how so?"

"Well, by adding that we are saying WrestleMania isn't good enough on its own, so we have to add a throw-in item to get fans to purchase it. Fans don't need that to purchase WrestleMania. It is the Super Bowl of professional wrestling."

"I disagree. It is going into the spot. End of discussion."

That was just one of many instances that marked the beginning of my end at WWE.

For my final commercial, for WrestleMania XIX in 2003, I defied their wishes, however. No cheap added bonuses — just pure emotion and heart.

This spot was filmed just a few months before I would decide to trust my own heart and leave the company. The words spoke volumes, to myself and others. And the images were stark and dramatic. First, here is the copy:

"We are all mortals.

"Our bodies, though strong, cannot defy time. One day, we will die.

"What matters most is the legacy we leave behind.

"Did we become all that we are capable of becoming?

"Did we make the difference we came here to make?

"Did we pursue our dreams, when all around us thought we were chasing illusions?

"Only those who dare to rise are able to lift themselves above horizons.

"Only those who chase dreams are the ones who catch them."

The voice-over was read by the award-winning actor Tony Roberts, most known for roles in a half dozen Woody Allen movies.

The eerie part was the visuals for the first three lines of copy. Shot at Tropicana Field in Tampa Bay, where WrestleMania would take place that year, the images featured Chris Benoit, Andrew "Test" Martin and Eddie Guerrero, among others. All three would pass away within a short time. On the line "one day we will die," Guerrero is shown sitting alone in a locker room with a solemn expression, his arms outstretched and head lowered, as if he'd had a premonition of doom.

Eddie died just over a year later. Hearing those words and picturing that lonely image of him still makes me uncomfortable to this day.

17

LEAVING WWE

"Kevin, I need to take a break. I need a sabbatical."

"Hah!" Dunn replied. "That's funny, Sahadi."

"I'm serious."

"Stop joking around. What's really up?"

"Honestly, I need to take a break." Dunn laughed again.

"Kevin, it has taken me nine months just to get up the courage to tell you this," I added. He still thought this was just a rib.

"Tell me you are joking."

"No, I am not."

"David, you have a great salary here. You have company-paid benefits and stock options. You got two bonuses just last year alone. Why would anyone in their right mind walk away from that?"

"I'm not sure, Kevin. My head says 'no' but my intuition says 'go.' It's just a voice I've been hearing in my heart for nearly a year."

"You really are serious, aren't you?"

"Yes, I am."

"Okay, well if you are really serious, how about I give you three months off with pay?"

"That won't work."

"Why not? It's more than fair."

"Yes it is. But then I will be counting down the days."

"Well how much time do you need off?"

"I don't know. It may be just two months. It may be six. I just don't know. All I know is I need to get away for a bit."

Dunn was silent for a moment, deep in thought.

"Kevin, I can leave in six months, or in six days, or the way things normally work here when someone is fired, I can leave in six hours if you wish. I know how it works around here."

"Okay," he replied as he looked at his calendar. "This is the first week in June. How about you stay on board for a month, until the first Friday in July, and then you can take your break?"

"That sounds great. Can I tell Vince the news now?"

"Oh, hell no!" Dunn said emphatically. "Something this big and of this magnitude . . . I need some time to figure out a way to break the news to Vince. Just don't tell anyone until I tell Vince first. Not even your staff. Promise?"

"Of course. Promise."

"One more condition."

"What's that?"

"On your last day, let's have a big party at the Redding Roadhouse that night."

I smiled with relief. "That sounds like fun!"

I left his office and started counting down the days until I'd leave WWE for however long I needed.

For the next three weeks I had to pretend it was business as usual, not telling my best friends at WWE or even my own staff. With just over a week to go, I flew to Los Angeles to shoot the final commercial I'd ever produce for WWE.

It was the aforementioned promotional spot for Summer Slam, featuring Brock Lesnar, whom I'd befriended on a shoot years earlier. Again, this commercial was a spoof of the movie *Jaws*: Someone yells "shark!" and the sheriff screams at everyone to get out of the water, causing a panic on the beach. In this version, as everyone is running away from the ocean, Lesnar suddenly appears in full wrestling gear, running *toward* it.

Halfway through filming, I noticed that the two behind-the-scenes camera operators — who were always present on these special shoots to document everything we were doing — had stopped filming and put their cameras down. "What's happening?" I thought. I walked over to ask John "Big" Gaburick, Kevin Dunn's best friend and the producer of the "Tough Enough" series, why they'd stopped shooting.

Gaburick smiled. "Kevin is about to gather the entire staff and tell them you are leaving us."

I was furious.

"What the fuck, Big? Kevin told me not to say a single word to anyone and now, while I'm in LA, he is telling the entire production team — and my own staff — about this, without me being present? Damn him! That's so fucking wrong. I wanted to tell my staff in person and he is denying me that privilege."

"That's just the way it goes sometimes," Gaburick replied.

"Well that's not right and you fucking know it."

I quickly walked away and then shouted a command to all who were present on set.

"Hey everyone," I said loudly so all could hear. "We are taking our lunch break now!"

I found a quiet place to call my top producer, Barry Bross, and tell him the news.

"Barry, Kevin Dunn is about to tell the entire staff that I am leaving the company. It's just a sabbatical though. I wanted you to hear it from me first, but Kevin forced me into silence, so please tell the entire staff the news before they hear it from Kevin."

"Why are you leaving?"

"I'll tell you later."

When the shoot was finished, I said thanks and hugged everyone who'd played a significant role. Thirty minutes later, I was given a ride back to my hotel. In the car were my producer Phil Spilker, the director of photography David Rudd, and the lead audio engineer. I sat, quietly, in the back. At this time of personal reflection, I didn't want to be front and center.

"Are you doing okay?" Spilker asked.

"I just need ten minutes of silence to let all of this emotion sink in," I responded. "There's a lot to digest."

They all obliged. We drove in silence. Just three minutes later, my phone rang. It was Kevin Sullivan, a friend and former producer on my staff who'd left the company months earlier. I thought he was calling to offer support.

"Hey Sully," I answered, as tears softly began to roll down my face.

"I heard the news, and I have mixed feelings," Sullivan said. "First, I'm happy you had the balls to finally do what you told me you were going to do nine months ago. But I also feel like you screwed me, because if I actually knew you would do this I wouldn't have quit WWE two months earlier, and I would have your job right now."

I wanted to say, "Fuck you!" But I didn't.

"I can't talk right now," I replied instead and abruptly hung up. What a cold, heartless bastard, I thought. Especially in this particular moment.

By the time I returned to Stamford to edit the spot, my departure was just days away. On one occasion Vince McMahon passed me in a hallway on his way to Kevin Dunn's office, which was three doors down from mine. McMahon was obviously angry and wouldn't acknowledge my presence or even glance my way. He walked straight past me as if the thirteen incredible years I gave him and the company, with all my heart and soul, meant nothing and had never even happened. Dunn had just recently told Vince the news of my imminent departure, so Vince probably assumed I had just given Dunn four or five days' notice, not four weeks.

And then I also realized why Gaburick was on the set for this spot. Big was learning from me. It would soon be known that Gaburick was Dunn's appointed successor for my position, even though he had no experience or an ounce of promotional creativity in his bones. Damn him. Big was a friend of mine, too. Damn them both.

On Thursday, my second-to-last day at the place I once so loved, Stephanie McMahon excused herself from a meeting and walked one flight upstairs into my office. She gave me a heartfelt hug and thanked me for all I had done and told me I'd be missed. Shane McMahon called moments later and wished me well, before adding, "And take your time . . . but come back soon!" I also called the executive assistants of both Vince and Linda McMahon to see if I could have ten minutes of their time to tell them in person my reasons for leaving, thank them for the time I spent there, and let them know I'd like to return one day. Linda's assistant responded immediately and told me to stop by in an hour. Vince's assistant gave me a blow-off line: "I'll get back to you."

I was very emotional when I walked into Linda's office. As I started to speak, the tears were trickling down my face before I could even finish my first sentence. Soon I was sobbing hysterically. Linda, the most gracious of all the McMahons, walked over and gave me a strong, loving hug to comfort me.

"Don't say anything right now, David," she said. "We love you and you will always have a home here. I am grateful for all you have done for us over the years. You've been a gem, a godsend. Take as long as you need, and remember you will always have a home here whenever you wish. I truly mean that."

I sobbed even harder. She was so loving and motherly, and still held me in her embrace. In that moment I felt like saying, "Okay, I'll stay." That's how much her care and comfort touched me.

"Thank you, Linda," I finally said as the thunderstorm of sobs eased to a light, lingering drizzle of tears. "I don't know why I have to take a break, but my heart is telling me to do so. And I hope to come back soon."

"David, you are family to us. And you can always come home. You are always welcome here."

Linda McMahon was the epitome of class. She always spoke genuinely and from the heart. And that moment meant the world to me.

On the other hand, Friday came and there was still no word on when I could say goodbye to Vince. I spent the morning exchanging goodbyes with my co-workers, then had lunch with my closest friends. At three o'clock I decided to leave. No point in staying, I thought. As I drove through the studio gates in Stamford and began my journey home, into an unknown future, I cried hysterically once again.

Ten minutes later my phone rang. It was Vince's executive assistant. I was six miles away.

"Vince will see you now."

"It's too late," I replied. "I have already left the building and I am not turning back."

I later heard that Vince told someone in his inner circle, "You know what happens to people who leave to 'go find themselves'? They wind up homeless on the street."

Over the next months and years, many wondered why I decided to leave an incredible job.

"He's creatively burnt out," Triple H would soon say, and in many ways he was right. The company I joined in 1992 was far different from the corporation I left. WWE went public, and they were beholden to their shareholders. I no longer had direct access to Vince. Instead I had to go through two layers just to schedule a meeting with him. And the company's many new "experts," who had gained fame in the world of television, knew nothing about the cult of personality that was professional wrestling. Where were they when I helped build an empire?

The new corporate executives that suddenly joined WWE were from the outside. They thought they knew better. Creatively, I was reeled in once again. Push the envelope? No chance in hell. They wanted to play it safe. It felt like I was back at NBC Sports.

And over time it became crystal clear that's the real reason I left.

18

THE SABBATICAL

The relief I felt that Friday when I quit my job at WWE was abruptly replaced by fear the following Monday morning. For two weeks, I would awake each day with acute anxiety. I have no job, I thought. What am I going to do now that I'm no longer receiving a paycheck?

My plan was to stay home for two weeks to gather my thoughts, get in shape and spend some quality time with good friends. Then I would go to Nantucket for another two weeks to indulge in everything imaginable, including sunny days on the beach, pub crawls by night, and flirting with the prettiest of girls. The anxiety was gone now that I was on this beautiful, blissful island just miles off Cape Cod, Massachusetts. I was about to embark on a spiritual journey, so I wanted to embrace a dash of decadent desires mixed with earthly pleasures beforehand.

I left my job because of what WWE had morphed into. But a deeper reason was revealed in the preface for the novel I began writing that summer, *Last Call of the Gods*.

> I needed a journey of spirit, of self-discovery and a need to gain deep insight in all that was truly important. What I truly knew for certain was that, like many of you, I was suffering from the soul sickness of modern society.

> We live in an age where there is a premium placed on the material. Our culture emphasizes youth, appearances and possessions. Our house is never big enough. We can always use more money and a new car. Each morning we awake, leap out of bed, and frantically jump back into the never-ending rat race. Our minds still spin like mice on a wheel when we sleep. If, that is, we can truly sleep. What we lack today is a profound belief system of enduring values like generations past.
>
> I had reached a point in my life where this world of pretense and superficiality had lost its appeal. I felt unfulfilled. My life was lacking purpose. I no longer saw the world through the eyes of a child, awed and inspired by the simple wonders of life itself. My soul needed to embark on this journey of discovery. My spirit longed for adventure. I was determined to find the true joy of life.

As I began my cross-country journey in my Jeep Grand Cherokee, loaded with everything I thought I would ever need, I had no agenda. Intuition was my road map now, my heart my trusted guide. I would drive as long as I wanted by day, then find a small town to get a modest hotel room and walk to a local bar. If I liked the town, I would stay a few days. If I didn't, I would wake up and leave the next morning. I also hiked in nearly a dozen national parks that found me as I drove unknown routes that changed daily, if not hourly. These national treasures were beyond beautiful, so peaceful and calming, as I hiked and beheld amazing sights that seemed as if they were born of my imagination. My favorites were the Badlands of South Dakota; the Grand Tetons in Jackson, Wyoming; Crater Lake in Oregon; and Yellowstone National Park.

On my way to Yellowstone, I stopped in the small town of Lander, Wyoming, checked into a motel and walked two blocks to the Lander Tavern. It was a cozy little place and had a great vibe. When I took a seat at the dark oakwood bar, the bartender approached me.

"What brings you to Lander?" she said with a smile as she placed a coaster in front of me. "Or did it just get in the way?"

"It just got in the way," I playfully said, returning her smile.

"That's what they all say."

After I sipped a few ales, I decided to engage the local patrons. They were fascinated by my cross-country journey, so I bought them all a drink. When the night was ending, an elderly Native American who was sitting on the far side of the bar signaled me to come over. And I did.

"So I hear you've traveled far," he said.

"Yes I have," I replied. Pride was talking now. "I've driven two thousand miles by car, and I'm going to drive another thousand miles to California to see the Pacific Ocean. Then I'll eventually get to Hawaii."

"Two thousand miles. So that is far, you think?"

"Absolutely."

After a slight pause, he pointed a finger to his temple. "The longest journey you will ever make is from here to here," he said as his finger traced a line down to his heart.

Wow! A light bulb went on, the brightest one I ever felt in my soul. That was my epiphany. I always trusted my intuition, my gut feelings, my heart over my head, no matter how hard that was. Now this kind, wise stranger was giving affirmation to my dreams, validating my beliefs, reinforcing that which I always knew but, enslaved by the corporate world, mostly ignored.

A month later I finally made it to Northern California, and just north of Crescent City I beheld a wondrous sight: the calm blue seas of the Pacific Ocean. I had done it! In just over two months I'd gone from the cold waters of the Atlantic to the warm and placid Pacific. Coast to coast, by car.

For three weeks I traveled down the Pacific Coast Highway. What beautiful sights I beheld. I made slight detours to Napa Valley to see a dear friend, Bob Caroli, who was one of my many voice-over artists at WWE, and eventually Los Angeles, where I visited friends I had worked with in my final months at the company.

After a week, I boarded a flight to Hawaii. I spent a month with Tantra Maat, one of the many spiritual teachers I met along my journey. I walked black sand beaches that were as soft as baby powder, and touched the sands of a pink beach as well as a green one on the Big Island. All looked surreal, but they were real.

When I left Hawaii I drove cross-country again, this time with an urgency. I traveled from Los Angeles to my home in Redding, Connecticut, in just five days. Soon I received a call from Kevin Dunn.

"David," he said, "I hear you're back in town."

"Yes, I am."

"Are you ready to come back to work?"

"I'm not quite sure. It's been five months and I'm still having fun."

"What are you doing tomorrow night?"

"I have no plans."

"How about we meet for dinner and drinks in Stamford and just talk?"

"Sounds great."

"Big will be there, too. I'll see you tomorrow."

The next night I met Dunn and Big at a restaurant bar. We had a drink before taking a seat at a table.

"Are you willing to come back to work for us?" Dunn politely asked.

"Maybe. What are my options?"

"I have five." Dunn explained all five, but each was just a slight variation on the others, and they all required me to report directly to Big, who I felt superior to. Shockingly, all would pay me half of what I was making at the time I left. I was not thrilled by any of them, so I had a counter.

"How about we start slowly?" I suggested.

"What do you mean by slowly?"

"What if I come back part-time at first, and we take it from there?"

"Define part-time."

"Well, hypothetically, what if I come back for just three months? Or six? I can come back to work on certain projects, just for starters, then we can reassess."

Big shook his head in a fashion that revealed he wasn't pleased.

"It's full time or no time," Dunn said. The cult that was WWE was still alive and well. The conditions for my potential return required complete surrender on my part.

"I can't commit to that right now," I replied. "I'm not yet ready for seventy-hour weeks again."

"Okay, then it's no time. Let's have some fun tonight like the good old days and get drunk. We can discuss this again in another month or two."

"Deal."

And like old times we did have fun that night.

A week later I drove to Boca Raton, Florida, to spend the winter with my beloved father. He was overjoyed. The time I spent with my dad was precious. While there, I put my house in Redding on the market. One month later we had an offer, and once the house was sold, I traveled to the Blue Ridge Mountains in North Carolina and ended up in the small town of Hot Springs. There I rented a modest place on a small river for two months and began writing *Last Call of the Gods*.

Then one day, nearly a year after I left WWE, an old friend called.

19

JEFF JARRETT

"Mr. Sahadi!" Jeff Jarrett said with glee and a distinct southern accent that was instantly recognizable. "It's been a while."

"Yes it has, Double J," I replied. His voice always made me smile.

"I hear you've been traveling cross-country for nearly a year."

"Yes I have!"

"Where are you living these days?"

"In a vacation rental just outside of Asheville, North Carolina."

"What are you doing there?"

"Writing a book, *Last Call of the Gods*."

"Have you been to Nashville yet?"

"No, I have not."

"Then why don't you come here for lunch on Monday?" Jarrett asked, which gave me pause. I suspected this had something to do with TNA Wrestling, which he'd co-founded with his father.

"Jeff, if I ever decide to get back into television it won't be for pro wrestling."

"Dave, let's just talk and see where the conversation takes us. Worst-case scenario is you can check Nashville off your bucket list of cities you have traveled to."

And so I went.

That Monday morning, driving through the Appalachian Mountains, I thought of my connection with Jeff. We first worked together on the music video "With My Baby Tonight" back in 1997. Jeff's gimmick at the time was a supposedly successful country music singer who had gained great fame in Music City. The initial vignettes that introduced the character were shot in Nashville a year earlier, at multiple renowned recording studios. For over a year Double J bragged about his successes, awards and accomplishments, but had nothing to back it up. His character was intended to appear a liar and a fraud — until we shot this video.

There were two locations where we would shoot. The first was in a dive bar in New York City named Manny's Car Wash. By "dive" I mean it had a dark, no-frills atmosphere. It was also an iconic local spot that showcased some of the best blues bands in the country. It was really a little-known gem. Celebrities such as Robert De Niro and Bruce Willis would often be sitting alone in the shadows, enjoying the atmosphere, the music. It was a hidden refuge from their fans. Once I even saw Willis get on stage and play three songs with his harmonica. The crowd knew who he was and applauded loudly while he was onstage in the spotlight, and left him alone when he returned to his seat in the dark. That's why they were regulars. No autographs to sign, no posing for pictures, but get onstage and perform every now and then if you wish.

I'd known the bar owners for three years. They were wrestling fans. On this night they gave us three hours for free before the main acts were set to take the stage, as long as we included a brief shot of the bar's marquee in the video.

As we were setting up, Jeff approached me.

"David, can I please get a beer to calm my nerves?"

"Of course," I replied. I knew one beer would be harmless.

Ten minutes later he asked for another. I obliged. By the time we began recording thirty minutes later, he and "The Road Dog" B.G. James had consumed six each. As he got on stage I was a bit nervous.

"Are you ready to roll, Mr. Sahadi?" he asked with a smile.

"Yes."

Instantly I was blown away. Jeff sang in perfect synchronicity with the track of a song that B.G. James actually sang. Yet no one could tell it was not Jarrett's voice. We did multiple takes with various camera angles, and Jeff nailed it each and every time. After midnight we went downtown to a recording studio and shot the song in black and white for intercuts with the live recording.

When the edit was done, it was a masterpiece. This low-budget shoot felt big time. And when it debuted on *Monday Night Raw*, the crowd that hated Jeff Jarrett was silent. He promised he would deliver a music video and dammit, after a year, he did. It's not what the fans wanted, yet it catapulted his character to a higher level. This con artist, this fraud, was suddenly legitimate.

As I continued my drive to Nashville that Monday morning, I also remembered the "Pissed Off" vignettes I did with Jarrett years later. Nothing compared to the fun and the magic of that night in Manny's Car Wash, though. I also wondered if Jeff would be pissed off if I said no to joining TNA Wrestling. I wasn't heading to Music City to hear Jeff's pitch as much as out of respect for the man.

When I arrived in Nashville, I met two leading members of CDHM, an ad agency from Stamford, Connecticut, in the parking lot outside of Cummins Station. While I was on sabbatical, CDHM had paid me a location fee several times to use my house as a set for a commercial shoot while I was away. It was also part of the guise on why I was visiting Nashville. Jeff and his father Jerry were keen on hiring me. President Dixie Carter, however, was not.

Present in the meeting room that day were Jarrett, Carter and her right-hand man Andy Barton. The ad agency gave their pitch on why they would be an ideal promotional machine for TNA, even though that was Dixie's job at the time. No one in the room seemed impressed. Then Barton, a senior vice president, turned to me and asked a question.

"David, how would you market TNA Wrestling?"

I was caught off guard. This wasn't a job interview for me. I was simply introducing TNA to an ad agency and catching up with Jeff.

"It's exciting, fresh and new, and has some of the most gifted wrestlers in the world, especially the X Division," I immediately replied. "So I would focus on the energy, electricity and the high-flying moves that no one else in the wrestling business is doing. TNA is unique. It is 'wrestling reinvented,' as Jeff would say, so I would promote it as the new evolution of professional wrestling."

I'm not sure where that spontaneous answer came from, because I was winging it. The response came *through* me, not from me but from a higher source, I felt. Looking back, I think it sounded convincing.

Jeff pulled me aside after the meeting was over.

"I want to have lunch with you and you alone. Not them. I am not interested in hiring an ad agency."

"Okay," I replied. So we went two floors down to an Asian restaurant on the first level of Cummins Station. Dutch Mantel, Jeff's right-hand man on all things creative, joined us.

"David," Jeff said, "I don't need an ad agency. I need *you*. Will you join us?"

"Let me think about it."

"Here's what's happening. We are launching our first three-hour monthly pay-per-view in November. It's called 'Victory Road.' I'd love you and you alone to produce the ad campaigns, promo spots and the opening video for the show."

I heard the passion in Jeff's voice, felt the deep love in his heart, the belief in his soul. I was touched. So I didn't have to think very long to help this visionary, this man I truly admired. My answer was instant.

"How about I join TNA for three months to help you launch Victory Road," I replied. "And when those three months are over we can reassess everything."

"That sounds like a deal."

Jeff was delighted, as was I. In that moment I felt needed and had a professional mission again. Part time. On my terms. I was resolute in my goal to help a flailing, upstart company gain relevance, to help Jeff's vision come to fruition. Much the way I'd felt a decade earlier when I joined WWE at its lowest of lows and helped them become a global phenomenon.

"There's just one problem," I told Jeff.

"What's that?"

"Dixie already told me that although she greatly admires my work, TNA can't afford to hire me just yet."

"Don't worry," Jeff replied. "I'll take care of that."

And he did.

I returned to Nashville a week later and produced a two-minute teaser spot that would end the very last, two-hour live broadcast from "The Asylum."

This was also the first time I attended the live show in person. What stands out to this day is not the show's matches but the enormous energy of the crowd. TNA was an alternative to WWE, a brand these fans truly loved. They were boisterous, loud and proud.

What also stood out was the vibe of the talent roster. They were eager, passionate, and willing to do anything and everything to make this company succeed.

When the word got out, WWE was not happy. The entire production team was assembled and told not to speak with me, that I was a traitor, even though it was just a part-time, three-month gig — something I'd offered to do for WWE several months earlier, but they refused.

"Aren't you pissed at Sahadi?" John "Big" Gaburick, the man who replaced me at WWE, asked a fellow producer, Doug LeBow, during lunch one day. (Against the company's wishes, Doug always put friendship first and secretly called me and told me of this conversation.)

"Why would I be?" LeBow asked.

"He's taking food off our tables."

"C'mon Big. We are fifty times bigger than they are. I'm glad he has something to do, and he's doing it on his own terms."

"He should have come back here," Gaburick insisted.

"He was willing to come back when you and Kevin asked in December, but Sahadi wanted to ease back in and work part-time at first, just like he is now for TNA. Kevin and you demanded that it had to be full time or no time. You had him and you let him slip away."

"He screwed us."

"No he didn't. You played hardball."

Two months later I delivered an epic cold open for TNA Wrestling's Victory Road. It was narrated by Barry Scott, a local voice-over artist in Nashville who I had never heard of before. His deep, commanding voice would soon become beloved by wrestling fans around the world for over a decade. It could make anything he narrated seem like the most important event in the world and reminded me a lot of a young James Earl Jones. He was gifted with the best voice of any narrator I ever worked with, and that includes many great announcers at NBC Sports and WWE.

Here is the copy of the opening, which was set to dramatic music and a ton of imagery:

"Life is not a random series of events.

"We cannot control the capricious moods of Mother Nature, nor slow the hands of Father Time.

"But as dreamers, we can build legacies, create new worlds, forge indelible moments that echo through time.

"For a company on the precipice of greatness, tonight is one of those defining moments, a chance to show the world the dream has truly become reality.

"But it is also a night for individual dream chasers, men of courage and passion, mighty warriors who train and battle and dedicate their lives in a quest to define their own enduring legacy."

The copy then went on to extol the virtues of "The Phenomenal" A.J. Styles, "The Alpha Male" Monty Brown, "The Charismatic Enigma" Jeff Hardy, and Jeff Jarrett before getting deep again:

"The stories are endless.

"Warriors, dreamers, men who have sacrificed everything for this chance at stardom.

"Tonight, boys will become men, men will become warriors, and warriors will take great steps on the road to immortality.

"These are their faces. This is their moment.

"Tonight, a genesis is unfolding. A brave new world is arising.

"Welcome to a new era of professional wrestling."

Jeff Jarrett asked to see it for the first time on the day of the event. When it was finished, tears rolled down his face. He was grateful beyond belief. In words, dramatic imagery, and what sounded like the voice of God, this cold open spoke his dream into creation.

"This has always been my vision," Jeff said. "This opening to the show just brought it to life. Thank you, Dave. Thank you."

Thirty minutes later, all of the talent on the roster, as well as the entire production crew, were asked to gather around the ring in the studio. When all were present, Jeff asked the television production truck to play the opening of the show on the big screen in the soundstage. As it played, not a single soul spoke or looked away. When it was finished, they erupted in thunderous applause, wide smiles on everyone's faces. They had never seen anything like this in TNA before. Jeff, the master motivator, knew exactly what he was doing. He wanted to infuse the entire roster and crew with hope and leave them no doubt that this night was truly going to be special, the beginning of a new era in professional wrestling.

Later, when the show began, I was in the audience. I wanted to see and feel the reaction while surrounded by fans. It was astounding. They were silent at first, yet quickly captivated. These loyal fans and their imaginations, their dreams, their hopes and their love for this company made them believe this show was an event-horizon moment in professional wrestling. As it ended, they roared and chanted, "TNA! TNA! TNA!" louder than I had ever heard before. At that moment, I knew this was the start of something special.

Those who truly know Jeff Jarrett absolutely love him. Myself included. He was one of the greatest people I ever worked for. His enthusiasm was contagious and his energy boundless. He had a bold vision that, although grand and at times elusive, was not unattainable. He created a tremendous backstage atmosphere for both talent and production, and when both facets of a company are in complete synchronicity with each other, it's only a matter of time before success follows.

"The vibe then was cool," TNA original Frankie Kazarian later told me. "It was really the last days of the Wild West. You had established former WCW and ECW talents, established independent stars, and new guys coming up like myself, trying to make a name for themselves."

Jeff Jarrett was an inspiration to all who ever worked for him. We'd all run through a brick wall out of admiration for the man and his vision.

I loved working for Jeff in the early days of TNA. He was a boss on paper but a friend in both work and life.

20

COOKIES AND BALLOONS

It was supposed to be harmless. A mere publicity stunt.

The footage we wanted to capture at Universal Orlando would be innocuous, just one facet of a package I wanted to produce so that TNA could broadly boast about the biggest weekend in company history.

Sadly, it was anything but harmless. And the aftermath brought great hurt to many, none more than my beloved father.

In November 2004, TNA Wrestling presented their first-ever monthly pay-per-view event, Victory Road. Their initial two-hour live event, which had aired weekly each Wednesday for two years, had run its course and ended in early September. Profit-wise, the show was a losing proposition — great idea, but not one that would ever make money. Victory Road was their first attempt to play with the big dogs and try to become a real competitor to WWE.

Days before the premiere, I received a phone call from a good friend who still worked at WWE in Stamford.

"Did you know we are shooting a commercial at Universal Studios two days after your event?"

"No, I did not."

"Well, you didn't hear it from me. Just wanted to let you know."

"Hmm . . . I might want to make some hay of this."

"That's not why I called you. Do not do anything stupid."

"I won't, but it could be some great PR for TNA if we get some shots of WWE superstars arriving at Universal Studios."

"Are you sure you really want to go that route?"

"Why not? I work for TNA now."

"I know, but if you make a scene you'll never work here again."

"I never want to work there again after the way they treated me when I joined TNA for just a short three-month deal, and they told all my close friends like you never to have contact with me again."

"Be careful."

"I will."

When we said goodbye, the idea was born. I was always told never to burn a bridge, but this was a bridge I never wanted to cross again, so I had no problem taking a chance and daring myself to create something special for Jeff Jarrett and TNA.

To put things in context, that weekend was TNA's first, major, three-hour pay-per-view. Both Hulk Hogan and "Macho Man" Randy Savage were backstage, curious and politicking, trying to gauge the vibe of what TNA was going to be as it entered uncharted waters, and so we filmed them as they watched the event keenly. And now WWE was coming to shoot a commercial two days later. Everything was aligning, I thought, and if combined those three things would be a perfect trifecta! The goal was to make a great press release and promotional video. I wanted to position Universal Studios, the home of TNA Wrestling, as "the new epicenter of the professional wrestling world!" We would intercut images of our event with shots of Hogan and Savage, as well as stars of WWE. With the blessing of Jarrett, I was granted permission to give it a shot.

The idea of "Cookies and Balloons" was both silly and benign. I would stay in Orlando, Florida, another day with "The Monster" Abyss, Konnan, B.G. James, Ron "The Truth" Killings, Shane Douglas and the first-ever TNA Knockout, Traci Brooks, and we would welcome the WWE to our home there.

Abyss would be at the front gate passing out balloons to all the stars and executives arriving in shiny black limousines. Traci would enter the green room dressed in a very sexy outfit and offer warm cookies to the bigwigs.

Signs of "Welcome to our Home" would be taped to the walls. And Bill Banks and Jeremy Borash would capture both their arrival and reactions on camera.

This was all simply designed as a PR stunt for TNA Wrestling to maximize our exposure and internet buzz. The day before the event, my production assistant Jess Ward and I were taping signs on the walls of the green room when the executives at Universal Studios discovered our scheme and confronted me.

"David, please take those signs down right now," I was ordered by the head of production at Universal. "WWE are clients, too. Know that, and respect that."

She was right. And so we did. As we took down each sign, another idea came to me.

There was no reason we couldn't do a shoot inside our own soundstage that day. I would pass it off as a "talent ID shoot" to Universal. All of our names were put on the sheet at the gate to gain access. The day of the WWE shoot I had the doors to Soundstage 21 opened, and we placed signs in convenient areas that said "TNA studios this way" with a red arrow pointing our way. We were trying to entice any curious minds on the WWE roster to wander over and take a glance at our stage. It would be captured on film. This was our "home-field advantage."

We were hoping there would be many. But on the day they arrived, there were none.

We waited five hours. Five long, anticipatory hours. Unfortunately, no one dared enter. They were obviously warned in advance that we may have devious intentions. We were all disappointed.

"They are not going to come over," I told the crew. "They've been warned, but I have another plan."

"What's that?" Banks asked.

"Do you see those tables and chairs between their soundstage and ours that are being set up now?"

"Yes."

"They are being set up for catering. That's common ground."

"What's the plan?" someone else asked.

"We can't go into their soundstage, but we are allowed to go there. So when they come out for their lunch meal, let's discreetly have the cameras rolling while Traci passes out cookies and Abyss offers balloons." They were so eager.

When the masses finally came out to eat, we took a stroll with cameras rolling. To our dismay, it was just dozens of freelance crew members dressed all in black who had no idea who we were. Not a single WWE superstar was among them. The talent had been kept inside and had catering delivered to them in fear they might be caught on camera if they strayed out of their soundstage.

Roughly ten minutes later, John "Big" Gaburick came out to confront me.

"Stop this now, David," Big demanded.

"We are allowed to shoot here," I calmly responded. "It's common ground."

"I thought we were friends."

"We still are."

"I order you to stop now."

"Order? Big, you can't order me to do anything. I don't work for WWE anymore."

His eyes filled with rage. If cameras weren't recording all that was happening, I'm sure he would have knocked me out with one solid punch to the face. He was that big, that menacing.

"You are dead to me!" he eventually said.

We all walked back to our soundstage. We were disappointed. We never got any footage of consequence, except for a quick glimpse of Rey Mysterio popping out of the door to the soundstage for a brief moment to say hello to Konnan.

Five minutes later, a production assistant from WWE came to our studio. I recognized her immediately.

"David, Vince and John want to talk to you right now."

"Where?" I asked.

"In our soundstage."

"I am not going in there alone."

"Why not?"

"I don't feel safe after what just transpired. Can I bring someone with me?" Shane Douglas, Konnan and Abyss were chomping at the bit to escort me there.

"No. They want to talk to just you. Alone."

"I promise we will not bring a camera with us. I just want some witnesses and protection."

"No. Just you alone."

"Then tell them I'll meet on common ground, out here in public so that we have witnesses. There will be no cameras. You have my word."

She turned and headed back to their soundstage to deliver the message. Shane Douglas was ready for a fight if things were to get violent. Abyss, too. I barely knew these TNA stars that wanted to protect me, but now I respected them greatly.

A few minutes later, the production assistant returned.

"They will not meet you on common ground," she said, "but they told me to tell you that if any of that footage airs anywhere, your ass will be sued."

Sued? My plan was never malicious. I just wanted to get some great publicity for TNA. And although we didn't get the footage we wanted, we sure as hell got even greater PR than I could have imagined. Their reaction to what we attempted to do made the moment appear more nefarious and bigger than it actually was, so the wrestling websites seized on the story. That alone was probably better PR than our original plan.

From that moment on, all of the friends I had left at WWE were forbidden to contact me in any way — and now with the added threat of getting fired immediately if they tried. No calls, no texts, no emails. I was devastated.

On the flight back to Nashville later that day, Bill Banks, a producer for TNA, was sitting in the row directly ahead of me. He turned around and gave me a fist bump.

"Thank you," he said. "You took a big risk and you probably burnt every bridge you have to ever work there again. You proved you are one of us now."

The next day I received a call from one of my former prodigies at WWE. He was hysterical, filled with rage and anger as he cursed me out incessantly. I let him vent for three minutes. His last words were "Fuck you."

"Can I explain?" I asked.

"No. Fuck you!" Then he abruptly hung up.

A month later, when my three-month deal was finished, Jarrett asked if I wanted to stay.

"I'd like to spend some time with my dad for the holidays," I told him. "While I'm there I'll mull it over and get back to you."

Soon after I arrived in Boca Raton, I told my father what had happened with WWE at Universal Studios.

"That's so sad, my son," my Poppa remarked. "That's not right." Then a moment later he became solemn. The magnitude of the event fully sunk in, and now he feared for himself.

"I hope they don't cut off my monthly paychecks."

"They won't do that to you, Poppa," I reassured him. "You worked for both Vince McMahon Senior and Junior. That would be an injustice."

For years McMahon had my dad on a "legends" contract. It was $3,000 per month, and it meant the world to him. It was a contract that would pay him for the remainder of his life. His only other sources of income at this time were his monthly Social Security checks and a few small book deals mixed in.

The next day his WWE check came. My father opened the white envelope, took out the check and went into an adjacent room. He placed the check on the soft carpet, knelt down and kissed it three times while making the sign of the cross. He did not know that I quietly witnessed this sight. He was thankful, but I was sad. My intuition is always right, and I had a sickening sense that this might be the last check he would ever receive from them.

Sure enough, Kevin Dunn called my father a few days later.

"Lou," I heard Dunn faintly say on the phone as I listened close by. "I hate giving good people bad news, but because of budget cuts we are stopping your legends checks. Financially we are in dire straits."

Bullshit.

To his credit, my dad was gracious and even went so far as to say he was thankful and truly enjoyed working for the company for four decades. But his heart was crushed, which made me furious.

What Dunn told my father was a lie wrapped in a smile that hid the true, devious intentions.

Two days later, I got a secret call from a confidant at WWE who told me he was in Dunn's office when a handful of people were gathered and a question was asked.

"How do we get back at Sahadi?"

There was silence for a moment, I was told. Then someone spoke with a devilish smile and evil intent.

"Let's hit him where it will hurt the most," he said.

"Where's that?"

"He loves his father dearly. Let's stab Sahadi in his heart by convincing Vince to terminate his dad's monthly legends checks."

That's what they did to get back at me: hurt my father. Reprehensible. Now I was beyond irate, but instead of returning anger and hate toward WWE, I decided to help someone else.

The very next day I called Jeff Jarrett.

"Jeff," I said, "we agreed to reassess everything after the holidays. Well, it's been just a few days and I have already made a decision."

"What is that?"

"I want to come back and work for you again. Maybe even full time. Do you still want that?"

"Hell yes!" Jeff shouted. "When do you want to start?"

"The first week in January."

Jarrett was overjoyed. I was empowered, on a determined mission fueled by personal and professional intentions. I also promised Jarrett that I would help TNA try and get a legitimate, weekly prime-time television deal on a major cable network.

Four months later, I did.

Game on . . .

21

THE SPIKE TV DEAL

When I returned to Nashville in January 2005, TNA was producing only two shows. One was the monthly, three-hour pay-per-view events like Victory Road, which we first launched in November. The other was a one-hour weekly show, *TNA Impact!*, that aired on Fox Sports Net at three o'clock on Friday afternoons. That deal was set to expire in June.

Fox Sports Net never paid for the show. Instead, TNA paid Fox $30,000 a week to air *Impact!* It was really just an hour-long infomercial intended to bring awareness to TNA on a legitimate sports channel. To make a profit, the commercial time was split between Fox Sports Net and TNA. Fox was able to sell their spots to advertisers, mainly because they were a renowned brand and had an established ad sales team. TNA? Barely anything, mainly because no one at TNA had experience selling commercial spots. In essence we were losing almost $30K a month for a minuscule number of eyeballs — if they weren't working or napping on a Friday afternoon at three o'clock, then perhaps they might see the show if they had nothing better to do. Our one-year deal with Fox Sports Net would end in June, and it would not be renewed.

But everything suddenly changed in April of that year.

WWE announced they were not renewing their deal with Spike TV and as of October *Monday Night Raw* would be returning to the USA

Network. The executives at Spike TV were devastated. *Raw* was their highest-rated show, and they felt the deep pain of betrayal. They had been a great partner for WWE, but WWE covertly landed a better deal from USA.

Upon hearing the news, I sensed a golden opportunity.

"Get us a meeting with Spike," I told Jeff. "I know people there from my time at WWE. I'll get us a deal."

It was a warm spring day in Nashville when Jeff, Dixie Carter, a consultant for TNA and I boarded Bob Carter's private jet for not one but two meetings. Chicago was our first stop, at 11 a.m. The consultant had arranged a meeting with the top executives at WGN, one of the last big-time broadcast networks left. We gave them our presentation and they were quite impressed. I sensed they dearly wanted our show, but I also had a deeper feeling that Spike TV was the place we needed to be.

An hour later we boarded the private jet and headed to New York City for an afternoon pitch to Spike. Deep down I knew we had a great chance of landing a deal because they were still feeling the sting and hurt from losing WWE.

Upon arrival we were ushered to the elevator and taken to their corporate offices. When we entered the executive boardroom, we sat alone. I marveled at the fact that this boardroom was one of the grandest I had ever seen. A few minutes later two senior executives, Brian Diamond and Jim Byrne, entered the room. After cordial but seemingly cold handshakes, we all took a seat at the giant desk. The mood was somber.

"We are just waiting for Kevin Kay before we begin this meeting," Diamond said.

Kevin Kay was the president of Spike TV, and I wondered whether he was the same Kevin Kay who once worked for David Letterman on *The Late Show* over a dozen years earlier as a cue card assistant. While at NBC Sports I was an enemy to Kay simply because he had a mad crush on my girlfriend at the time, Deirdre Dod, who also worked for Letterman as a booker. Back then, Kay was jealous when Deirdre and I got engaged.

Ten minutes of awkward silence ensued, and then Kay entered the room. The instant we made eye contact, Kay smiled. It was a nervous smile at first, but he was happy to see me. He knew my reputation as a lead executive at WWE.

"So, it really is you, David," he said in a slightly embarrassed way that only I knew the reason behind. "I saw your name but thought it might be a different David Sahadi."

"It is really me. So good to see you, Kevin, after all these years."

I stood to shake his hand. He returned a hug. Perhaps it was Kay's way of saying he was sorry.

When we hugged, a palpable, collective sigh of relief came from the two executives at Spike. Now they were willing to engage us.

"So you are no longer with WWE?" Kay asked.

"Not anymore," I replied. "I left a year ago."

"I heard a rumor you took a cross-country sabbatical."

"That rumor is true."

"So are you fully in with TNA?"

"Yes."

"That's good to hear. Now tell me why?"

"I truly believe in the product and in this man's dream," I said, pointing to Jeff Jarrett.

"You know WWE screwed us, and we are a bit leery about getting into business with another company in the wrestling industry," Kay explained.

"I understand. And I left WWE well before they screwed you."

Kay smiled. Then he addressed us all.

"That being said, let me hear your pitch on why we should make a deal with TNA."

Jarrett stood and put on a masterful display. For nearly twenty minutes he spoke passionately, without interruption, though it felt like just five. I watched as the Spike executives became awed by Jarrett's energy and his grand dream. Then Jeff asked me to play the sizzle reel I had produced in Nashville.

It was a highly energetic and stylized two-minute video that captured the incredible athleticism of our athletes and had a look and feel that was different from WWE. The Spike TV executives were captivated.

"We are not WWE," Jarrett said when the video was done. "We are the alternative, a new brand bringing innovative ideas in our quest to reinvent the world of professional wrestling."

They were convinced, and so was I.

"We are highly intrigued," Kay said after the meeting. "Let's meet again next week and discuss this in further detail."

"That would be great," Jarrett replied.

"So you really are part of TNA now?" Kay asked me once again.

"Without a doubt." That made Kay smile. He knew the success I'd had at WWE and felt relieved that an experienced and talented producer was fully onboard.

The second meeting went well, and soon we had landed a new cable television deal with a big-time network. We would air on Thursday nights at 10 p.m., right after *WWE SmackDown* concluded.

During the months between the end of *Raw*'s tenure on Spike TV and TNA Wrestling's debut, I would cut TNA spots that Spike would air during commercial breaks in WWE programming. WWE was pissed because Spike was airing spots promoting a potential rival. I believe they knew I was producing those commercials, and that I somehow played a small part in landing this deal. Tough shit. There was nothing they could do to stop Spike from airing TNA commercials. WWE was a program soon to be leaving, so Spike was no longer beholden to their desires.

WWE was irate. We were excited. It truly was about to become a new era in professional wrestling.

I finally had my redemption. And vindication.

All because WWE screwed my dad for something he never had a part in.

22

TNA DEBUTS ON SPIKE

It was a historic night, one I'd never forget. And I wasn't even there.

I had remained in the Nashville studios to continue working on postproduction packages and bumpers. On Thursday, October 1, 2005, the very first episode of *TNA Impact!* aired on Spike TV from Universal Orlando. And a lot had changed in the months since we'd signed the deal with our new network.

That summer, I hired my former top producer at WWE, Kevin Sullivan, to become the director of postproduction. Sullivan was very talented, and his passion and care were always obvious. Even though his leadership skills ruffled a few of his staff, I wanted to hire him to handle the full-time, day-to-day activities of TNA postproduction because I wanted to remain an independent contractor. Also, I didn't want to deal with approving invoices, creating spreadsheets, and all the other mundane things that position required. I wanted to remain creative.

At first Sullivan rejected the notion of joining TNA, but Jeff Jarrett used his immense powers of persuasion to convince him to join. We were glad he did.

Dixie Carter was happy as well. I told her Sullivan was very talented but also a "bull in a glass shop."

"Good!" Dixie replied.

She wanted a bull in production to be a perfect complement to my positive, uplifting and inspirational attitude. It was classic "good cop / bad cop." Both are needed. With both, one plus one equals three.

(On the other hand, Sullivan wasn't hired to be my boss, but he acted like he was. Jarrett was my sole boss. More on that in chapter 27.)

In that summer of 2005, we also hired a new director, Michael Vetter, to replace the former director Mike Miller. Miller was very talented and had directed many shows for WCW during the Monday Night Wars, but he and TNA could not come to a financial agreement that summer. That was the three-month period when *TNA Impact!* was no longer on Fox Sports Net and before the big debut on Spike. Miller wanted to get paid per show he directed, which was the norm at the time, but TNA wanted to pay him per day while we aired only on YouTube. This meant he would only be paid once per month because we taped all four shows in a single night.

Enter Michael Vetter. Months earlier, Jeff and I had interviewed Vetter over a steak dinner in Nashville. Jeff and I were both impressed by his vision, his confidence and his thoughts on shooting the show, which required putting cameras in creative positions. I really liked him, and he got the job.

Vetter directed the first-ever episode of *TNA Impact!* for Spike TV, and it was a ratings success. The executives at Spike had been hoping for a 0.3 and would have been ecstatic if we'd reached 0.4. We doubled their expectations and delivered a solid 0.8! Over time, that number would grow. And TNA would grow.

But Vetter's time at TNA would be fleeting. Keith Mitchell, our television producer then, was not happy working with him. Mitchell saw his flaws and how they affected the production of the shows. The entire production team agreed with him. Mitchell relayed that to Jeff, who also thought the same. Then one day in December, Jarrett approached me.

"David, Vetter is not the director I hoped he would be. And the crew is not behind him. I want to make a change, and I want you to direct our shows beginning in 2006."

I was stunned. It was not something I'd ever desired to do.

"No chance in hell, Jeff!"

"Why not?"

"I direct commercials, talent vignettes and promotional campaigns. They are all one-camera shoots. Just like the vignettes and music video I filmed with you."

"Stop it, David," Jeff responded. "A director is a director. You can do this."

"There are different types of directors, and being a multi-camera director for a live show is something I have never done, nor do I want to even attempt. It's 'left-brain' thinking, using the rational side of the brain, not 'right brain,' which is creative."

"Please David. Just give it a try. I don't want to bring Mike Miller back."

I paused, then had a revelation that would save me from sitting in the dreaded director's chair. Most people in television production would revel at the chance, but I didn't in that moment.

"Jeff, I heard that Vetter is a great producer for college basketball. And Keith Mitchell can also direct. What if we get Vetter and Mitchell to switch roles? Let's give Vetter a chance to produce and see if Mitchell would be willing to direct."

For those who do not know, Keith Mitchell is the most famous, legendary producer in pro wrestling history. He started out as a camera operator for Jim Crockett Promotions in the 1980s, then quickly ascended to the role of television producer. Among his many accomplishments, he produced every show for WCW and then WCW *Nitro* during the golden era and the Monday Night Wars. When WCW was purchased by WWE, Keith helped Jeff Jarrett launch TNA and was the producer for nearly every TNA show until 2019, when he left to become the executive producer for All Elite Wrestling. Mitchell helped mold many careers, including mine.

The following day, Jeff, Kevin Sullivan and I convened in the conference room at the TNA offices in Nashville.

"Keith, I know you have directing experience," Jeff began. "Do you think you can direct the show better than Vetter?"

There was no delay. "I can direct circles around him," Mitchell confidently replied.

"Sahadi said he heard good things about Vetter as a producer for NCAA basketball. Before I fire Vetter, what if we try using you as the director and Vetter as the producer?"

"I'm okay with giving it a try. I just don't know how well he can produce anything, much less wrestling."

"Well, we will soon find out," Jarrett replied.

That experiment lasted less than two months. Our announce team, future Hall of Famers "The Professor" Mike Tenay and Don West, could not stand Vetter either and would often yell at him during rehearsals, commercial breaks, and even during live telecasts when we were playing a video package. Mitchell, burdened with Vetter's ineptitude, tried his best to both direct and produce, but those are two separate and unique roles, an impossible task for one person even to this day.

"Vetter is done," Jeff said to me in late February. "I'm going to fire him soon, and I don't want to bring Miller back. Will you at least give directing a shot?"

I was scared as shit, and Jarrett knew that. So he tried his best to calm me.

"It's a taped show," he said reassuringly. "Just give it a shot. We can fix anything in post."

So I acquiesced.

I was about to enter a new, foreign realm. Most directors work their way up from a grip to a camera operator and eventually the back of a television production truck before ultimately ascending to the director's chair. I never had that luxury, that experience. Instead I was thrown into the fire without ever having the singes of the flames of experience, of making mistakes, as one works their way up.

Fortunately I was blessed with a camera crew that liked me and wanted me to succeed. As well as the tutelage of Keith Mitchell, who took me under his wing and let me fall before teaching me how to rise again. Jeff Jarrett had faith in me, saw the potential inside and gave me the patience and the long leash I needed to rewire my brain to learn how to direct a multi-camera show that was taped live, not pieced together like my previous work.

I must also give thanks to Scott Fishman, our executive-in-charge, who was our liaison between TNA and Spike TV. A former director and producer, he also encouraged me and gave some great advice.

At first I was an average director at best. Then, with the help of so many talented professionals, I became a good one. Eventually, I'd be one of the best.

23

THE RISE OF TNA

The mid-to-late 2000s truly was TNA Wrestling's golden age. Each year, our ratings on Spike TV increased. Each year, superstars from WWE would join our roster.

Jeff Jarrett was the spirit, the puppeteer, the persuader behind all that was unfolding. His influence and positive attitude not only ignited the talent and crew, but also landed some big fish from big wrestling promotions.

Sting was one of the first. He signed with TNA in 2005 after turning down offers from WWE due to his lack of respect for the goliath of professional wrestling.

"I'll never work for Vince McMahon," he often told the wrestling media, and he told me the same thing.

Christian Cage would also join TNA that year.

In the spring of 2006, TNA had a match for the ages at the "Unbreakable" pay-per-view event. It was a five-star, triple-threat match, and Samoa Joe, A.J. Styles and Christopher Daniels gave it to them in spades. They dazzled the audience with their incredible athleticism, high-flying antics and death-defying feats. Dave Meltzer of the *Wrestling Observer Newsletter* was moved to give the match his highest honor of five stars, making it only the second American match to earn that distinction that decade. To this day, many people still see it as the greatest match in TNA history.

Taking stock, we had some stars as well as national attention. What we truly needed, however, was something money could not buy. That something was credibility.

Credibility finally came, and in a huge way. The biggest splash of this era was the surprise announcement that a multi-time WWE World Heavyweight Champion and future Hall of Famer, Kurt Angle, was coming to TNA. The announcement was made at the end of Unbreakable. It was a hype video that was shot a week earlier in Nashville at Marathon Music Works, now a vibrant music venue but then an abandoned building close to our downtown headquarters. At the end of the pay-per-view, the Angle video appeared on the giant screen to the audience present as well as hundreds of thousands of viewers around the globe.

"He is a former world champion," said Barry Scott, the iconic voice of TNA Wrestling, as we showed silhouettes of Angle training in a wrestling ring.

"An Olympic gold medalist, arguably the greatest wrestler in the industry today," Scott continued. The crowd began to cheer. The silhouettes revealed more and more of who the famous superstar was. Then we cut to a tight shot of a hooded person, and as he raised his head and pulled the hoodie back, it was revealed that it was indeed Kurt Angle. The crowd erupted.

"It's *real*," Kurt said, looking into the camera. "It's damn real!"

When the video ended, we cut to the ecstatic fans, who were amazed and overjoyed that Angle was joining TNA. The announce team of Mike Tenay and Don West loved it, too.

"Can you believe it?" Tenay shouted in disbelief. "Kurt Angle is coming to TNA!" Neither announcer knew that until the video aired. Everyone had been sworn to secrecy.

Sting was there when we began shooting the video a week earlier. He had no idea Kurt Angle was about to arrive. Sting believed we were just shooting dramatic scenes of his dark persona for use in promos, video packages and opens. We could have told him, but we wanted to catch him by surprise. When Angle did finally arrive and make his presence known, Sting was truly shocked.

"Kurt Angle! Is that really you?" Sting asked gleefully.

"Yes, it's me. I just signed a contract with TNA."

"Kurt Angle is actually in TNA!" Sting shouted into the air.

Kurt then looked around the set and saw me.

"David Sahadi?"

"Hello Kurt."

"So good to see you again. Are you directing this shoot tonight?"

"Yes, I am."

"This is fantastic!" he said before giving me a strong, Olympic-caliber hug. Kurt was later asked how he felt when he first saw me that night.

"I immediately felt so at ease knowing TNA had signed an MVP for our production," Angle replied. "David Sahadi came up with masterpieces when he worked at WWE."

It's amazing to this day that this monumental moment was never leaked anywhere until the video appeared on the big screen. Everyone kept silent, Sting included, even though keeping a secret that big is nearly impossible in the wrestling world.

Angle's in-arena debut came on an episode of *TNA Impact!* on October 19. Marching out with great purpose, Angle entered the ring to confront Samoa Joe. They stood face-to-face in the center of the ring, staring each other down, their heads just inches away. Suddenly, Kurt delivered the "headbutt heard round the world." Down went Joe. The crowd roared in delight. Then, as I cut to a tight shot of Angle celebrating, magic happened. A bloody Joe arose just behind Angle without Kurt noticing, an unplanned moment that can never be recreated. When Angle turned, Joe delivered a devastating muscle-buster to the Olympic gold medalist. The pull-apart brawl that ensued was electrifying and would set the stage for Angle's incredible, decade-long run as a top main eventer for TNA.

"There have been some amazing moments in TNA history," Cultaholic Wrestling would write on their website, "but they don't come much better than Kurt Angle 'laying the nut' on Samoa Joe."

Prior to Angle, the company's biggest mainstream star was Christian Cage, who had never even made it into a major pay-per-view event in WWE. Now, TNA had signed a man who had main-evented WrestleMania and was universally respected and adored by the fan base. Kurt Angle was the last piece to the puzzle. TNA had arrived.

In the fall of 2008, Samoa Joe was riding high, and so was TNA. With his mentor Kevin Nash now guiding him, Joe was destined to have a rematch with Kurt Angle at "Bound for Glory." But first, Joe had to go through Sting. Joe was unintimidated and obliterating Sting — until there was a classic swerve. Kevin Nash unexpectedly turned on Joe, causing Sting to win the title.

The following night, Nash, Angle, Sting and Booker T came together for a very entertaining backstage segment. The Main Event Mafia was formed and became one of the greatest factions ever in professional wrestling. TNA would never be the same.

Noting that they were out to get respect from the roster's younger members, the Main Event Mafia soon recruited Scott Steiner to their faction. For nearly a year, they would run roughshod over the entire TNA. They were always dressed in designer suits, as if mocking the younger TNA Originals that were the foundations of the promotion when it was first launched in 2002. At one point the Main Event Mafia would hold all of the TNA Championship gold.

Many other renowned superstars would join TNA as well: "The Charismatic Enigma" Jeff Hardy, former WWE heavyweight champion Mick Foley, and Mr. Anderson to name a few.

The wrestling world was taking notice. TNA was rising, and so were our ratings.

24

SEX, LIES AND POWER PLAYS

The rise was fast — and so was the demise.

In the summer of 2009 TNA plateaued, and "what could have been" would never happen. The fall began suddenly, and all because of rumors, lies and power plays.

For reasons many knew two years earlier, though most pretended not to, it was quickly obvious to all. I never thought it would progress to the point of calamity, but it did.

The drama and rumors first started in 2007. Word got out that Jeff Jarrett was dating Karen Angle, Kurt's wife, many months after Jeff's beloved wife Jill succumbed to breast cancer. TNA President Dixie Carter confronted Jeff about the rumors, which he at first denied before reassuring Carter that the relationship was over. Carter seemed convinced, perhaps even relieved.

But the story wasn't over.

In 2009, a TNA employee anonymously called into the *Bubba the Love Sponge* radio show and declared that Karen Angle was in a long-term relationship with Jeff Jarrett and had moved in with him, along with her children and Kurt's. It was indeed true. However, it was deviously spun as a story of Jeff "stealing" Karen from Kurt. Jeff never did.

I knew most of what was going on but told no one. I had seen Karen at Jeff's house earlier that year while doing a shoot, so I knew they were an item even before Dixie Carter did. Jeff had no intentions of hiding it from his trusted few, and later not even from Dixie.

What remains a mystery to this day is why it was spun that way — who was that caller, and what were their intentions?

When the story came out, Dixie suspended Jeff for lying to her. The scandal was an opportunity for Carter, one she had wanted for years. Now she finally had a legitimate reason to oust Jarrett from the very promotion he'd co-founded with his father, Jerry Jarrett, and Bob Ryder in 2002.

The truth is far different from the rumors most of us were first fed. Nearly a generation later, in 2023, Jeff would come clean on a podcast with Conrad Thompson.

> I want to set the record straight here. Me stealing Kurt's wife is the furthest thing from the truth. The fact of the matter is when we hired Kurt Angle — and I say we, me and Dixie Carter, because she's a part of this story — they [Kurt and Karen] were legally separated. They weren't living under the same roof . . .
>
> The whole world thinks, oh yeah, you got sent home because of that whole disaster and Bubba the Love Sponge or whatever it was. No, the fact of the matter is Dixie Carter, for the third time, pulled a power play. She tried the first one during my wife's illness. The second one was about twelve months later. The third one was during this, and I gave her the rope to hang me. She went to her father and said, "Oh, we can't have this." She didn't give two shits about Kurt Angle. She wanted to power-play to run the tale . . . and in twenty-four months, she put the company in a financial death spiral, so her power play essentially put [the company] out of business.
>
> Vince Russo's absolutely a part of this. Vince's whole plan was to go along with it. He knew damn well. He knew damn well the Kurt and Karen situation. He knew absolutely all of

> it. He sat on the sidelines just like Kurt — "We're just gonna let Jeff sit home." Guess what? Jeff's just trying to put his life back together? No. Let him sit home because Vince Russo's plan was, I'll get Jeff out and I can write the show by myself.

In an interview in 2009 with Howard Stern, Kurt Angle admitted that he had been "cheating on Karen" during their separation in 2007 and that Karen was dating another wrestler at the same time as a means of getting back at him. That revelation gave credibility to Jarrett's claims.

Professional wrestling is a world of factions, secret coalitions and covert liaisons. Jeff Jarrett wanted both Keith Mitchell and me to resign in protest when he was suspended. That was something neither of us would consider. Yes, we were loyal to Jarrett. Yes, Jeff was a dear friend. But I was hoping this would be a temporary suspension, and I still had to take care of my father, who was struggling financially after WWE canceled his legends checks. So I did my best to help bring Russo's creative ideas to life, since he had complete control over creative.

Since I didn't resign, Jeff may have thought I was a Dixie Carter loyalist. But in Dixie's mind I was still one of "Jeff's guys." Russo wasn't quite sure where I stood, and he never asked. Because of that my voice lost a lot of its influence. I paid a steep price. My sole loyalty at this time was to TNA and whomever their head of creative was. In fact, that is always where my loyalty resided. In Jeff's absence, I was just trying to be Switzerland, neutral to all sides, doing my job to the best of my abilities. In most professions that is a good place to be whenever there is a massive shake-up or a restructuring in leadership. In the world of professional wrestling, however, that meant I was beholden to no one, and that's a bad place to be. It means you are a potential threat.

Taking the high road, Jarrett would return a year later and flip the so-called scandal into a storyline feud with Kurt Angle. But he no longer held backstage power; Carter had made sure of that. He was used simply as a performer, with a minor role in the office.

In the fall of 2010, Jarrett turned heel and became a founding member of the Immortal faction. His stated mission was to get back at Dixie Carter for taking away all of his power in the company he started. Art imitating life.

From there, Jarrett set his sights on Kurt Angle, and the two began to feud over their real-life issues. Life imitating art.

Really, only one person paid a big price in 2009: Jeff Jarrett himself, the man who hired me and inspired me, who asked me to join in 2004 and allowed me to make great change and present TNA as the alternative to WWE, as a new era in professional wrestling.

What disheartened me equally was that long before Jeff returned, Carter would rid TNA of various backstage staff who were loyal to Jarrett, including booker / creative writer Dutch Mantel. I was saddened. Dutch was the one responsible for booking the TNA Knockouts Division with great success. Dutch's departure was not only a loss for the *Impact!* product, but I lost an ally.

Without the full trust of anyone, I was alone, wandering in nowhere land.

25

HULK HOGAN ARRIVES AT TNA

There was a rumor he was coming. Then the rumor became reality — he was here.

In November 2009, it was announced at a major press conference in New York City that "The Immortal" Hulk Hogan — the most famous and beloved professional wrestler of all time — was joining TNA Wrestling in January.

I was both excited and anxious. Hogan was an icon and this was an epic announcement that would get the attention of the world. Hogan would bring a lot of eyeballs to TNA. At least at first.

With Jeff Jarrett sidelined, and Dixie Carter having ultimate power now, there was no stopping the inevitable. The publicity would be dynamic, the attention of the pro wrestling world focused on us. The only question was, would this be good or bad for the future of TNA Wrestling?

For one person, this news was bad. Very bad. Vince Russo, who was given ultimate control over all the storylines and all things creative just months earlier after Jeff was sent home, would lose his stroke.

Eric Bischoff, who attended the Hogan announcement, was perceived as the evil one during the Monday Night Wars, when Bischoff's WCW nearly put the WWF out of business. With fortitude and determination, the two goliaths of wrestling mightily fought. While at the WWF, we spent over a year trying to tear Bischoff and the WCW down. After eighty-three weeks, we finally did, and at great cost. Now Bischoff was at TNA, and I would have to work with him.

When I first met Eric Bischoff on the set of the Impact Zone, all fears were allayed. The demon was just an illusion, like a scary monster in a child's mind. What a great, genuine guy, I thought at first. And for three years we had a wonderful relationship and gained great respect for each other.

On January 4, 2010, Hulk Hogan's long-awaited arrival came on Monday night TV. TNA decided to go head-to-head with WWE *Monday Night Raw*. The press was electric and the fans were eager to embrace some real competition, hoping this night would trigger a seismic shift in the world of professional wrestling — the start of the Monday Night Wars, Part Two. And on that magical night, TNA Wrestling delivered.

The ratings for both shows increased. On Spike TV, TNA delivered its highest numbers ever, a 2.0, which had peaked in the first hour at 2.2 when we were unopposed by *Raw*. Hulk's arrival in the Impact Zone was surreal. When he walked into a TNA ring for the very first time, the crowd chanted "Hogan! Hogan!" and "TNA! TNA!" with great fervor. Hulk didn't speak for nearly two minutes because the roar of the crowd was relentless.

"Words could not do this moment, and this reaction, justice," Mike Tenay, TNA's play-by-play announcer, said between the chants. The crowd was euphoric.

"We are making history tonight!" Hulk Hogan finally said, then described the great change that would be happening.

Scott Hall and X-Pac, former members with Hogan in the New World Order group a decade earlier, were sitting ringside. Eventually they stood and entered the ring. They pleaded their case to be part of the change. Then Kevin Nash's entrance theme played and he entered the ring as well. Things started to get heated, then Eric Bischoff walked out. He confronted the former members of the nWo: They, like everyone else, would have to earn their place in TNA. When they left, Bischoff asked for the formats for that night's show. When he was handed them, he tore them apart and pulled another format from his back pocket.

"That was tonight's format. And you get an 'A' for effort, but this is the format now." He handed it back to the ringside stage manager and said, "Give that to your director."

In an instant, the game had changed.

Sting watched all that was unfolding from high above in the rafters. Soon, "The Charismatic Enigma" Jeff Hardy would make his long-anticipated return, Rob Van Dam appeared, and later in the night a limousine arrived and out walked the legendary "Nature Boy," Ric Flair. What star power.

Nevertheless, Hulk Hogan's debut remained the big breakthrough.

"Maybe more so than any other moment in TNA history," wrote Ryan Meisner in the Bleacher Report in 2013, "this one caused people who had no interest in TNA . . . to start buzzing about TNA and what they might be able to do, or what their plans might be.

"It was a hotly hyped moment that went astray later, but for that moment, as Hulk Hogan walked down the ramp to the ring in the Impact Zone, everything was right in the world."

Wow, we are legit competition now, I told myself. Or so I thought.

In March of that year, the decision was made to go head-to-head with WWE on Monday nights in an attempt to rekindle the Monday Night Wars of the late 1990s. I was adamantly against the idea.

"Why, David?" Dixie Carter and other TNA executives asked.

"Because they will destroy us," I replied.

"No they won't. Our talent roster is as good as theirs."

"I don't deny that."

"Hulk Hogan and Eric Bischoff both believe it would recreate the magic of the Monday Night Wars of the nineties."

"It was a different era."

"David, look at our ratings on Monday night when we went head-to-head with WWE in January."

"That was an anomaly, the Hogan Effect."

"Then why do you think it is a bad idea?"

"WWE is live in big arenas that hold roughly 15,000 people. We are in a soundstage studio that holds only 600, 700 at the most. The fans that are clicking back and forth will notice that."

"I disagree," said another executive. "They will be focused solely on the talent in the ring."

"The talent in the ring is irrelevant if we go head-to-head," I persisted. "Yes, we have a superb and gifted group of athletes, but it's all about the optics. The audience will click back and forth and WWE will look like an expensive Ferrari in their huge, sold-out arenas with 15,000 cheering fans, and we will look like a worn-down Volkswagen Bug from the early seventies with way less than a thousand fans in attendance."

"It doesn't matter."

"Yes it does. Optics mean everything on television."

Despite my objections, the decision went ahead. With Dixie Carter having final authority after she sidelined Jeff Jarrett a year earlier, my opinion mattered little to them. I no longer had Jeff's ear, nor he the final say.

I was hoping I was wrong, but my premonitions proved true. In the first weekly head-to-head airings, we got trounced. And even worse, *TNA Impact!* lost half of its loyal viewers from Thursday night. For the next seven weeks, the ratings would drop each week, until we hit rock bottom with a 0.5. That's when panic set in.

"What the hell are we going to do?" Dixie Carter frantically screamed over the speakerphone in the corporate conference room where Sullivan, several executives and I sat.

"Let's ask Spike to move us back to our old time slot on Thursdays," her most trusted ally suggested.

"Does anyone else have another idea?"

Her ally muted the speakerphone and angrily said, "We should just fucking fire Hogan and Bischoff. They are fucking bleeding us dry, and they have Dixie's ear."

Then the phone was unmuted.

"Let's move back to Thursdays," another responded.

Really, we had no other choice.

The name value of Hulk Hogan was still high in 2010 when he was signed to a major deal with TNA. However, Hogan's reputation for attracting controversy wherever he went continued with TNA, which ran into many issues due to his presence.

And there would be casualties.

"I was very excited about the opportunity of working with Hulk Hogan,"TNA superstar Cody Deaner would later tell me. "I'm a child of the early to mid-eighties. I was a Hulkamaniac. He's the reason I wanted to become a professional wrestler since the age of five. I was excited to not only meet my hero but work with him."

Then something happened to Cody. He got released three weeks before Hogan arrived.

"I was told I was released in order to make room for some of the guys Hogan wanted to bring in," Cody said. "So I went from the highest of highs to the lowest of lows. I went from the possibility of working with my hero to getting fired because of my hero. That was a tough pill to swallow."

Eventually it would be clear that Hulk Hogan's arrival marked the beginning of our demise.

26

THE HOGAN/BISCHOFF ERA

In the spring of 2010, *TNA Impact!* went head-to-head with WWE *Monday Night Raw* again. We got our asses kicked. Badly.

"He's like a carton of milk," I remember Triple H saying about Hulk Hogan several years ago. "There is an expiration date."

Despite the colossal failure of our challenging WWE on Monday nights, it was still an exciting time in TNA. That is, if one believed the carton of milk to still be fresh and half full, not half empty. Fans, and some talent, were enamored by the possibilities of what we could become. Many were not. There would be more casualties.

Hulk was a great hire, but in my opinion one who should have stayed just a few months, not a few years. He was well past his prime, and his body, battered and scarred after three decades of wrestling, performance enhancers, and constant travel from city to city, would not allow him to do much physically in the ring. His role at TNA Wrestling was mainly limited to pre-tapes and in-ring promos.

"He's like a carton of milk" continued to echo in my head. I knew the shine would wear over time. Yet Dixie Carter, against everyone's advice, kept extending Hulk's contract. Three months became a year, and then another two years after that. Hulk, Bischoff and their cronies were getting paid so much that Cody Deaner and other talents in TNA Wrestling were either getting fired or forced to take pay cuts. Myself included.

"The Hogan/Bischoff era was great," Kurt Angle would later tell me. "But I think the company put lots of money on the line to sign Hogan and Bischoff. That's a pricey signing."

"After my release," Deaner recalled, "I watched what the Hogan/Bischoff era tried to do with the product and the changes they made. I personally felt that the majority of those changes resulted in stripping TNA of its identity and what made TNA unique as an alternative brand to WWE."

Yes, we were becoming "WWE Lite." Hulk Hogan had the freedom to call the shots, and it rubbed many TNA Originals the wrong way. They remembered Hogan saying negative things about the company's past, as well as some of the talents that were still there. A rift was created in the TNA locker room, one that later became a major fault line. On television, our product was morphing into something we were not. As Deaner said, we'd lost our identity.

Eric Bischoff, however, I thought very highly of — and still do. That revelation will surprise a lot of the people who have so many negative things to say about Bischoff. Did he make a lot of money over the years, especially at TNA? Absolutely. But what's wrong with that? Professional wrestling is a business, after all.

What I admired most about Bischoff was that he always had a great mind about the business, about branding, about building storylines and their arcs. With Eric there, we would actually do walk-throughs with TNA talent once again during the day, and he'd always ask my opinion on certain segments, as well as on the "blocking" of the talent. There were times I'd suggest something new and different to him. Sometimes he would like the idea; sometimes he wouldn't, but then he would have the decency to explain to me why. Yet Eric always listened. He showed me tremendous respect, and that's why I have so much respect for him and all he has done in the business. After all, if he hadn't challenged the WWF when he helped launch WCW *Nitro*, and eventually beat us in the ratings for eighty-three straight weeks, the WWF would never have risen and become the behemoth it is today. And the new era did indeed spark some great storylines and ideas.

One success story was the creation of the biker faction Aces & Eights. It would go on to become one of the most polarizing storylines in the history of *Impact!*. A group of marauders wearing masks while dressed in biker gear, Aces & Eights would attack anyone and everyone on the *Impact!* roster. The angle ran in 2012–13, at which time they became the new rulers of this domain.

For thirteen months these masked assailants would leave cryptic messages with their soon-to-be victims and then suddenly attack them at random, whether it was backstage, in the ring, in the parking lot, and on occasion even in their hotel rooms. This group had a single mission: They were hell-bent on destroying everything. One reason why the angle worked so well at first was because it brought a sense of unpredictability and paranoia to everyone who was not a member — the members wore masks to protect their identities, thus making it easy for wrestlers to become distrustful of one another. Storyline-wise, that's just what they did.

Highlights include an all-out brawl that took place at many locations all over Universal Studios. The clash ruined the wedding of Bully Ray and Brooke Hogan, and led to the shocking reveal of Bully Ray being the Aces & Eights president the entire time after pretending to be their adversary and eventually winning the Impact World Championship. The fans were enraged. They threw bottles and other objects into the steel cage, while Hogan and his daughter Brooke were screaming outside the walls in disbelief.

The group would become bloated after the reveals of Garett Bischoff, Wes Brisco and D-Lo Brown, and the inclusions of Brooke Tessmacher and MMA superstar Tito Ortiz. But the overall angle was one of the best creations of the Hulk/Bischoff regime.

In my opinion, an equally great creative idea was the making of Bobby Roode, a long-time fan favorite, into one of the most detested heels in TNA history in a single night: the night that Roode became the TNA World Heavyweight Champion.

Roode was supposed to beat Kurt Angle on October 16, 2011, at Bound for Glory, a pay-per-view event that was shown live from Philadelphia. That never happened. Everything changed during the production meeting the morning of the event. As the format was being read out to all the agents and key productions, Eric Bischoff spoke up.

"Hey guys, hear me out," he said. "Terry [Hulk Hogan] had an idea last night. Just hear him out."

The room was mystified, myself included. Then Hogan rose and spoke.

"What if Kurt Angle wins tonight instead of Roode," Hogan said, "and then on the following episode of *Impact!* James Storm beats Angle and wins the title? Then we can have a match between the two beloved brothers of 'Beer Money, Inc.,' Storm versus Roode, out of courtesy and friendship, and suddenly Roode turns on his best friend and tag-team partner. Bobby Roode would become the ultimate heel, Storm would gain the sympathy of the crowd, and we would launch two rockets into the stratosphere instead of just one."

The room was silent, but I smiled. I absolutely loved the idea of taking two TNA Originals and elevating them both to main event status. It was a win-win for the talents and the fans.

For Bobby Roode, this would be the beginning of a glorious 256-day reign as the TNA World Heavyweight Champion, beating the likes of Storm, A.J. Styles, Jeff Hardy, Sting and Rob Van Dam.

Now back to the ugly side of the Hogan/Bischoff era.

Joey Haverford described the situation in an article in *The Sportster*:

> One of the strangest segments in TNA history featured a real-life meeting with Dixie Carter addressing the TNA roster after the news of Hulk Hogan joining the company. Many people were negative or just feared for their futures with someone getting full creative power to change everything that was going on.
>
> TNA filmed the segment with Carter running down anyone against the move and implying they should leave if unhappy. The roster was basically talked down to by Carter, all for a move that ended up badly failing.
>
> Hogan flopped leading TNA, and Dixie just alienated a large percentage of the roster.

In the summer of 2013, Eric Bischoff would leave TNA, and Hulk's departure would soon follow. I was sad that Bischoff was sent home because I truly liked his wrestling acumen and the respect he showed me. And I loved his brilliant and creative mind.

But I wasn't upset that Hulk Hogan was leaving. That carton of milk had expired long before.

27

BIG AND SMALL

For many years Kevin Sullivan and I would bicker over silly things that morphed into unnecessary bigger things. Even though he was my greatest hire ever, he was always the instigator. Sullivan thought he was my boss the day he started at TNA, but in reality he never was.

I spent weeks convincing Dixie Carter and Jeff Jarrett to hire Sullivan so that I could remain a creative, be on the road and eventually direct the shows, and not have to be in Nashville on a daily basis. I didn't want to sit in regular meetings, sift and sort through paperwork and supervise an entire production staff. Since I hired him to do what I did not want to do, how could he have possibly thought he was my boss? It annoyed and astounded me.

Sullivan wanted me to be in Nashville Monday through Friday, but I didn't live in Nashville. I lived in Chattanooga, Tennessee. And the deal I signed in March 2006 to become the director of *TNA Impact!* (and all of their live pay-per-view shows) included a stipulation: I would only be required to be in Nashville to assist with postproduction for ten days per month. Nothing more. It was my idea. I did not want to be beholden to Sullivan, his temper tantrums, his capricious moods and his military style of leadership.

No one knew what mood Sullivan would be in each day until he arrived. He was like Dr. Jekyll and Mr. Hyde. His staff members nicknamed him "Dr. Kevin and Mr. Sullivan." It was funny, and it was fitting.

Don't get me wrong, Kevin was a great friend. For two decades we created top-notch promotional campaigns, talent vignettes, cold opens and video packages together, for both WWE and TNA. And we had fun, especially when we weren't working — sharing a beer or three in Nashville and a bunch of laughs. I would work with him, but I just would not allow him to be my boss. Kevin was a great guy outside the confines of the office walls and always made friends and strangers laugh. Inside, he was someone different, often a terrifying monster. Many employees left TNA because of him.

I actually worked thirteen to fifteen days a month in Nashville, not ten. In my mind, I was giving TNA several extra days for free because I truly cared about our growth and wanted to build an empire. In Sullivan's mind, I was neglecting him all the other days that would have brought the total to twenty. And he did not consider traveling to Universal Orlando and directing shows as "working."

What could he not understand? I had hired him — for a larger salary than mine — so that I would have peace of mind. He got company-paid benefits; I did not. He viewed me as a full-time, salaried employee even though I wasn't on salary and still worked sixty hours a week on average. These spats we had would pop up every couple of months, but we would usually reconcile in a day or two with some beers at a local bar.

Then one infamous day in December 2012, it happened. It was the worst day possible for him to start another spat with me, a day that crossed a sacred line for the final time.

It was a sunny Friday afternoon, December 14. I had spent eleven straight days on the road, save for a one-night layover at home in Chattanooga to do laundry, rest, repack and go back to Nashville. The production crew, minus Sullivan, spent back-to-back weekends taping the holiday shows at Universal Orlando, and I was back in Nashville to help edit them. Then the news broke.

There had been a mass shooting in Sandy Hook, Connecticut. Twenty schoolchildren and several teachers were shot and killed, and dozens more wounded. As the production crew broke for lunch, I stayed in the Nashville studios to watch the news. This was personal for me. Sandy Hook was just a few miles from my home in Redding, Connecticut, when I worked for WWE. Every weekend I would visit the town to get a cup of coffee at Starbucks and meet friends. This moment really hit home — I thought of all the years I spent there, all the people I knew.

When Jim Morris, our lead editor, returned from lunch, I asked him a question.

"Jim, what's left to do for the show today?"

"All I have to do is put in the lower thirds for the talent entrances," he replied.

"How long will that take?"

"Oh, about two hours because of the rendering process."

"This school shooting is hitting me hard. I lived nearby. I feel a deep sadness in my heart. Would you be okay if I leave now?"

"Of course. I know how to spell Kurt Angle, and you can always check the spellings on Monday. We do not ship the show until next week."

"Are you sure?"

"Get out of here," he said. "I got this."

I continued listening to the news on my two-hour drive home. I heard the president address the nation. As he began to cry, so did I. It was then that I decided to turn my phone off and be alone with my thoughts.

Thirty minutes later, I turned it back on. I was not going to let this horrific moment ruin my weekend, and I wanted to console all my friends who were saddened and be a positive influence and give them perspective. Yes, I was going to be happy, to uplift and heal those who were sad.

What happened instead was I saw a text message from Sullivan.

"So do you get paid for a full day when you only work a half-day?" There was anger in his tone.

I was outraged. "I have a contract, and the conditions of that contract are not your fucking business," I texted back.

"Not my business? You mailed it in. You are a joke."

I threw the phone down. Goodbye Sullivan — friend turned asshole, again.

The following Monday morning I returned to Nashville. When I walked into edit room one, Sullivan was there working with Jim Morris on a graphic about this tragic event. I took a seat next to the *TNA Impact!* producer, Andrew Thomas. Although I was expecting an apology from Sullivan, one never came. He ignored me and I him. Until I spoke to Andrew.

"How was your weekend?" I asked Andrew. Before he could answer, Sullivan stopped what he was working on and turned to me.

"What did you say?" Sullivan asked.

"I was talking to Andrew, and what I said was personal," I sternly replied.

Sullivan rose and glared at me.

"I knew you would still be pissed when you got here today," he said in an angry, arrogant voice. "Just so you know, it wasn't me who questioned why you left early Friday afternoon. It was someone from the executive floor." Then he left the room and slammed the door on his way out.

"That is fucking bullshit," I told Andrew and Jim. "He means Dean Broadhead, and Dean would never say that. I'm calling Sully out." Dean was the CFO who'd helped craft my contract years earlier.

"I am going upstairs to ask Dean now."

I didn't have patience for an elevator. I raced up three flights of stairs to get to the executive floor. When I got to Dean's office, he was just arriving from his home in Monteagle, Tennessee.

After a quick exchange of hellos, I got straight to the point.

"I want to talk to you about Kevin Sullivan."

"Well that's funny, because I was just going to call you when I'd settled in and ask you to come up to talk about Kevin as well, so come into my office."

Dean opened the door to his office, gently put his overcoat on a coat rack and took a seat at his desk. He invited me to sit down as he moved folders and stacks of paper to each side of his desk. When he was finished, he looked right at me.

"So, Kevin Sullivan," he said, not really asking.

"Yes, Sully," I replied. He could sense I was upset.

"You go first."

"Dean, I left early on Friday because I was disturbed by the events that happened that day. I lived just over a mile away. Kevin implied that you had questioned why I left early. Is that true?"

Dean's smile dissolved into instant anger.

"*Damn Kevin Sullivan!*" he yelled as he rose, then proceeded to ferociously throw everything he had just organized off his desk and onto the floor.

"If I ever questioned your work ethic and desire I would ask you myself," Dean explained. "I never asked that. And I am sick of his daily bullshit. I have a folder here full of complaints from employees over the years who have felt they have been harassed by him and believe he created a hostile work environment. There is a potential lawsuit here. I want to replace him."

When he'd calmed down, I asked him a question. "So what did you want to ask me?"

Dean took a deep breath before replying.

"Have you ever heard of John Gaburick?" he asked.

I was stunned. Of course I knew who he was. I hadn't heard his name since the "cookies and balloons" incident, when he took part in getting back at me by screwing my dad.

"Do you mean 'Big' who works for WWE?"

"Yes, Big."

"I know him well."

"Well, we have been in negotiations with Big for a few weeks. I haven't told you before but I want to hire him to replace Sullivan. What are your thoughts on that?"

Wow. I was dumbfounded. And I had mixed emotions. Big had been one of the few present in Kevin Dunn's office when they canceled my dad's checks years earlier, and this came out of nowhere, but I told Broadhead the truth.

"Well, he's not very creative, in my opinion, but he is a tremendous manager and a talented producer."

"That's what I wanted to hear. We don't want to hire Big to be creative, but to just manage the postproduction department. Half of the staff wants to leave because of Sullivan's behavior."

"Well, he would be a good manager. That's all I can say."

The sad thing is that I loved Kevin Sullivan as a friend, and still do. And he's incredibly talented. But in that very moment, angered both by his texts on Friday and lying to me that morning, I couldn't come to his defense. Not then. If the incident had happened weeks earlier, or days later, I would have made a case for Sullivan to stay. I could not argue for keeping him now if TNA had already lined up someone else to replace him, and had a folder that justified firing him — even though I thought the alternative was not a good choice either.

It wouldn't matter. Dean and the powers that be had already made their minds up weeks earlier, unbeknownst to me.

For some reason, change did not come for a while. It was not until the beginning of June that Sullivan got fired and John Gaburick became his successor. The delay could have been due to a no-compete clause that prevented Big from joining TNA right away. Or perhaps the final details of his contract were still being negotiated.

When the news finally broke that June, I was asked by many why Big was coming to TNA and what his role would be.

One June night in Las Vegas, after Sullivan had been fired and Big was taking a vacation before joining TNA, I met Hulk and Eric Bischoff in Hogan's suite. Over drinks they asked why Gaburick was coming to TNA. I told them what I was told by Dean, which I thought was the truth at the time.

"He's just replacing Kevin Sullivan in postproduction," I reassured Hulk and Bischoff. "He is not a threat to anyone in live TV production or in creative."

"Are you sure?" Bischoff asked, not fully convinced.

"That's what I was told by Dean. That's all I know."

As I mentioned earlier, I had tremendous respect for Eric Bischoff and truly enjoyed working with him all those years. I would never lie to Eric. In a world were backstage politics are deeply entwined in the fabric of the business, I was a rare babyface in a world of heels.

It soon became clear, however, that what I said was not the truth. And it took just a couple of weeks for Gaburick to reveal his true colors.

Bischoff would recall the events years later on his podcast, *83 Weeks*.

> As it was presented to me, Big was going to oversee all of television production. It made sense because John was very involved working under Kevin Dunn. The product could have been better. John was a guy who could take it to the next level.

> I was all for it, and I was one of his biggest fans. John called me and told me, "I'm just coming in to help and really see what I can do on the television side of things." I was like I couldn't wait for him to get there, brother. For the first few weeks it was that kind of vibe. But it became obvious pretty quickly that John was interested in more.

One day that summer, Dixie Carter wanted Bischoff to go to Dallas with Gaburick for a meeting with Bob and Janice Carter. Her parents, the owners of Panda Energy, were helping to finance TNA at the time. At first Bischoff tried to avoid the meeting.

"I didn't interact with Panda at all," Bischoff revealed. "Intentionally, I tried to avoid it. I made it clear in my contract that I was not an employee. I was basically a consultant and executive producer for a television show and would eventually show up as talent. I didn't want to discuss business issues."

Eventually, Bischoff went to Dallas because he was a team player. He loved the passion and energy Janice had. At the end of the meeting, however, Bischoff realized why he'd been asked to go.

> The reason I was called to be there was because there was a desire to restructure TNA and they wanted me to report to Gaburick. Which, number one, would have been a change to my contract because that was not the way it was set up. Number two, I went "Umm, no!" Not that I didn't like John, but no.
>
> We got out of that meeting and I remember we were getting ready to get in the car for the airport, and John goes, "Eric, this is going to be great! Right?" He knew that Janice wanted me to report to him. I told him that wasn't going to happen. I'm not doing it. I'm changing my relationship with the company because the company wants to restructure and I don't want to report to you. It's just not my thing. That was pretty much the end of it, and shortly thereafter I was on my way out.

Eric wasn't the only one on his way out. Soon after, Hulk Hogan, Bruce Prichard and Jeff Jarrett would be gone, too.

I felt horrible. I had endorsed Big as the head of postproduction. Little did I know I was lied to. Little did I know I'd sold these great leaders a bag of lies. I felt betrayed, and I felt like I had betrayed Eric Bischoff and Hulk as well, even though I did not.

John Gaburick wanted power. And now ultimate power was what he had.

28

FREE FALLING

When John Gaburick first arrived in the summer of 2013, TNA Wrestling was already on a downslide. Our audience was diminishing, the critics were becoming more vociferous and the locker room was a mess. The mood was bleak. A sense of dread permeated every facet of the company.

One year later, things got even worse.

In the summer of 2014, Spike TV declined to renew our contract, which was set to expire in October of that year. Besides the declining ratings, their main concern was about trust. Or a lack thereof.

The network had asked over a year earlier that Vince Russo be removed from any creative aspect of TNA. They were told Russo had been fired, but it was a lie. A misguided email, possibly leaked, had Vince Russo's name on it, and it became clear to all of Spike's executives that Russo remained an integral part of writing and orchestrating the storylines. The network executives felt betrayed. How could they not? I was on their side.

Many would say one of Dixie Carter's worst decisions kept coming back to haunt her. It was Dixie who decided to keep bringing Vince Russo back. Russo was polarizing. His approach to booking storylines and wrestling shows was erratic, and his presence caused a rift between Jeff

Jarrett and his father Jerry, one of TNA's co-founders, who was present at every TV taping in the company's early days.

After leaving TNA in 2012, Russo was secretly rehired, and when word got out that he was working for the company again, we ended up losing our TV deal with Spike.

"I don't know if I could pinpoint an exact time when things began to go downhill in TNA," Frankie Kazarian would later tell me. "I always try to focus on my job at hand, but obviously I would always hear and see things. I know constant management changes didn't always sit well with talent. By the time I left in 2014, the team they had in place running things was not, in my opinion, fit for the job."

In January 2015, TNA's *Impact Wrestling* debuted on the Destination America cable TV channel. It was doomed from the start. At a hotel bar in December, an executive from Destination America overheard a disparaging comment from Dixie Carter about the president of the network.

From a production standpoint, I was no longer the television director in the truck. Big had decided to use the handheld cameras "untethered," which meant there would be no cables connecting the cameras to the truck and really nothing to direct. The camera operators were now their own directors. Every single match would be edited by myself and a production crew in our Nashville studios. This was pitched as a way to be "innovative" and "unique." That also was a lie. It was merely an attempt to save money on production costs, since the rights fee we were getting from Destination America was far less than what Spike TV was previously paying us.

The deal lasted only one year. By October we were searching for a new cable TV partner and finally found one: the Pop channel, which was another downgrade.

In 2015, *Impact Wrestling* had some bright spots but was not a going concern for many wrestling fans, who had an embarrassment of riches in terms of quality in-ring content to pay attention to. While NXT, Lucha Underground and New Japan Pro-Wrestling were impressing fans, *Impact* was just delivering one embarrassment after another.

That summer, Billy Corgan of Smashing Pumpkins fame joined TNA. The news that a beloved rockstar was helping steer the *Impact* ship certainly got more attention than anything else the show was doing at the time. Corgan became the senior producer of creative and talent development, and eventually the president of TNA Wrestling.

Corgan was no stranger to the wrestling business, appearing in ECW and running his own promotion in Chicago's Resistance Pro Wrestling. And Corgan brought a different layer of creativity to *Impact*. The show became strong and consistent and had some memorable storylines. A notable one was the creation of "Decay," a bizarre yet compelling faction of misfits that was loved by the fans.

Another was the "Broken Matt Hardy" saga, perhaps the crowning achievement of Corgan's run. Other wrestlers flourished, too, with the Decay faction notably feuding with the Hardys, and Bobby Lashley finally becoming the top guy he'd been expected to become for years.

Later that winter and into the spring, many TNA talents decided to leave, confused by the conflicts between the many parties in charge. My favorite wrestler of all time, Kurt Angle, was one of them. I was sad.

Angle would tell a reporter that every time his contract ran out, TNA had a new one lined up for him to sign. The future Hall of Famer was making seven figures a year at TNA, while most of his peers, Hogan aside, were making barely $100,000. Angle also had a sense that with the company's financial issues, they may not be able to afford him much longer.

Angle said he loved every aspect of TNA, from the television tapings to the house shows and his fellow locker room talent, but he knew the promotion was almost "at the end of the rope."

"I left TNA because I wanted to go back to where I started, in WWE, to finish my wrestling career," Kurt would tell me. "But I loved TNA and had some amazing moments there."

Kurt Angle left TNA in the early part of 2016. It would prove to be a year of infamy.

29

ANTHEM PURCHASES TNA

In my view, 2016 was notable for only one thing: deceit.

It was well known that TNA Wrestling was losing money. Lots of it. They were also losing market share and networks, who were dropping TNA amid diminishing ratings each year. Bob and Janice Carter, who had helped fund TNA since it lost its original investors way back in 2002, stopped funding their daughter Dixie's enterprise in 2014. Though the bonds of love are strong between parents and their children, business is still business. Investors do not like to lose money, and after twelve fruitless years neither the Carters nor Panda Energy had received a return on their investment. They knew they were funding a losing effort, so they finally bailed.

In the fall of 2015, financial aid came from Aroluxe, our production company at the time. Led by owner Jason Wike and his two generals, Ron and Don Harris, they funded the company for several months. In early 2016, after investing over $2 million without a return, they turned off the tap in exchange for a large share of the company.

Enter Billy Corgan. In 2016, Corgan used his own money to pay for three sets of television tapings. He had dreams of one day purchasing TNA and molding it into his own, unique version of professional wrestling. In August of that year, Corgan became the promotion's new president, while Dixie transitioned to chairwoman and chief strategy officer. It was all just a ploy, an insidious strategy wrapped in a lie.

Corgan was led to believe he was the real president of TNA Wrestling, but soon he would find out he had no real power at all. In an alleged attempt to extract Corgan's money, Dixie Carter had used her powers of manipulation to fool Corgan, later telling him and others that he was merely the president of TNA on TV, in character form only. This really pissed Corgan off.

I wasn't aware at the time, but reports surfaced that Canada's Fight Network, through its parent company Anthem Sports & Entertainment, had also acquired a stake in TNA. Three separate entities were partially funding the company throughout the year, and all three had plans to take over TNA in the future. In wrestling terms, it was a triple-threat match, and I would like to say I had no horse in the race — but that would be a lie. I was rooting for Aroluxe. Why? Because while TNA was six months behind on paying my postproduction fees (money I'd never see), Aroluxe was still paying my director's fees.

Plus I was good friends with the former tag team the Harris Twins, Ron and "Heavy D," as I would call his brother Don. I loved the Harris brothers. They were the ones who had returned me to the TV director's chair a year earlier, just five months after John Gaburick's untethered-camera plan proved to be an unmitigated disaster.

Still, I went about the business of doing my job as best I could, staying silent in the shadows while the three goliaths battled it out on the business side.

On November 3, TNA announced that Anthem Sports & Entertainment had provided a credit facility to fund Impact Wrestling (as TNA would be rebranded) and that Corgan had been removed as the promotion's president. Corgan would soon reveal that neither TNA nor Anthem had repaid the $2.7 million debt still owed to him by TNA. Corgan threatened to sue as well as convert the debt into a 36 percent stake. Anthem took the high road and agreed to a settlement with Corgan and TNA, Anthem acquiring the loans Corgan had made to Carter in the process. What a mess.

30

FURLOUGHED OR FIRED?

The phone call came early one afternoon in late November. I didn't recognize the number.

"Hey David. It's Scott."

"Hello Scott."

"With me on this call is Ed Nordholm."

I knew then that this phone call would not bring good news.

"David, you know how much I love and respect you, and I hate to bring you this news," Scott said. "This is the toughest thing I have ever had to tell a person I admire and love, but we are letting you go. Michael Vetter is here again and has been working behind the scenes helping us try to get our budget in order, and he doesn't see the need to pay for an independent director. He is wearing five hats for us in this critical moment, and he offered to direct our shows for free as well, as part of his contract."

"I understand," I solemnly replied.

"This has nothing to do with you. Your skills and expertise are second to none. It's just an attempt to save some money for now."

"I get it, Scott. It makes perfect sense from a business perspective."

Then Ed interjected, "I want to thank you for all the hard work you have done for us, and I truly respect your talents. Please understand this is just business, nothing personal."

"I totally understand, Ed. And I wish you both luck. I love the company, don't want it to fail, and I hope everything works out."

In truth I was pissed. Not because it was the first time I was ever fired in my life, but because TNA had cooked the books when they sold the company to Anthem Sports & Entertainment. At the time, TNA was grossly in debt. Bills were stacked up, and many would never be paid. TNA still owed me nearly $33K when they sold the company. That was money I knew I would never see. I was just hoping that forgiving the debt, and the sins of the previous regime, would endear me to the new ownership. But it did not. They didn't know. How could they? They were lied to. The numbers and accounting that were presented to Anthem added up at first glance, but not for long.

It's been said that when TNA closed the doors of our offices at Cummins Station on 10th Avenue in downtown Nashville, they owed half a million dollars in rent to the landlord, which also would never be paid. The janitor we loved was not paid for the final six months of his life as well. He was just one of many, like me, who'd invested passion, care, hard work and pride into an idea we deeply believed in, not knowing we were being played and betrayed.

Despite my initial bitterness, I saw opportunity. I knew my skill set and creativity were second to none, and I wouldn't have difficulty finding another job. If I wanted one, that is. At first I didn't. Having the luxury of being comfortable financially, I was in no rush. I viewed this as my second sabbatical, albeit one that was brought upon me, and I looked forward to new adventures.

For a month I traveled through the scenic Blue Ridge Mountains of North and South Carolina, hiking by day before finding a small town and a local bar to down a few pints. That really put life into perspective once more, just as it did in 2003 when I left WWE. Eventually I drove to southern Florida to spend some quality time with my beloved dad.

When I returned home to Chattanooga, I decided to get a part-time job as a server in a local restaurant. I was writing both a book and a television series called *Bar Wisdom: Lessons on Life, Love and Hangovers*. And I came close to being a television star with my own weekly series.

Bar Wisdom was similar in concept to the popular CNN series *Parts Unknown* with host Anthony Bourdain. Instead of visiting restaurants,

I would travel to various cities and discover local bars that were hidden gems, and both gain and impart wisdom while I was there. The latter part was the book version. After two meetings with executives of the A&E network in New York City, the television series was nearly picked up. The concept was a finalist, but wouldn't make the final cut.

In the spring of 2018, I also began directing shows for Major League Wrestling (MLW), co-owned by Court Bauer and Sean O'Haire. They were a smaller promotion than Impact Wrestling at the time, but the vibe was eerily similar, in a positive way. Once more I was trying to help a beleaguered company rise again, as when I joined TNA in 2004.

I am a builder, not a destroyer. I'd rather help build a brand or a company than just join one that was already wildly successful. And when it came to MLW, I saw the potential in the way it fused different types and styles of professional wrestling. Although the production values were very limited, the ring was center stage and the athletes that competed in the squared circle gave it their all every night. For die-hard fans it was perfect.

Court Bauer adored me, and I respected the shit out of him as well. Court also paid me a very handsome fee to direct their shows. I felt welcome, so I gave more than they expected. I helped in every way possible. MLW was truly my family at this time.

When MLW first called me to direct shows at the Melrose Ballroom in Queens, New York, in April 2018, I called my dad. He was ecstatic. His son was back in the limelight of television production.

A week later, the day before I flew to New York, I called my dad twice. He didn't answer. That was odd, and I was concerned. Finally, on my third attempt, he did pick up, but he sounded "off."

"Hello, my son," he said in a weak, raspy voice.

"Poppa, are you okay?"

"Yes. I'm just watching basketball."

"You sound tired."

"I am."

"Are you sure you're okay?"

"Yes, I'm just tired. Don't miss your flight tomorrow to New York."

"I won't Poppa. I love you."

"I love you more," he replied, his customary response.

I didn't know it at the time, but he wasn't okay. He was in the ICU when I called but didn't want me to know. He wanted me to get on the plane to New York in the morning and direct those shows for MLW. He knew it was important to keep my career alive. My father lied to me, but only out of selflessness and love for his son.

When I landed in New York the next day, I got a call from his girlfriend, Susan. That's when the truth was revealed.

"Your father is in the hospital," she told me.

"What? I just called him last night."

"I know. He was in the hospital when you called. I was there, too. He didn't want to tell you because he just wanted you to go to New York and not worry you. He knew that you would not go to New York if you knew the truth."

"I'm flying back now."

"Do not. He just had a minor heart attack and they are putting a stent in tonight. It's a simple procedure."

"I'm flying back right now."

"Please do not," Susan said. "He will be fine, and I am with him. He wants you to direct those shows for MLW. Please do what he wishes."

Words cannot describe how I felt in that moment. A myriad of emotions were hitting me at once. Confusion, uncertainty and sadness were all evident in my face. People noticed. I was overwhelmed.

With a heavy heart I informed Court and Sean about what was happening. They implored me to go, saying they'd try to find someone else to direct those shows.

"I got this," I said. "It's what my dad wants me to do. I will not let him down."

"Are you sure?"

"Yes. He would be disappointed in me if I left."

That show would be the first of many I would direct for MLW over the course of nearly two years.

Many people have said bad things about Court Bauer. I am not one of them. I felt his passion, saw his desire. I wanted to help and he welcomed my help. And he truly cared about my father, even though he'd never met him.

"You did a wonderful job," Court texted me a day later. "Our TV show has never looked better. Thank you for all your hard work.

"It's been a real pleasure having you as part of our team. I'm looking forward to working with you again in Milwaukee in June and would enjoy finally getting a chance to have a proper conversation with you. Perhaps we can jump on a call next week?

"Hope your father is doing better."

That's what I loved most about Court. Every time he called, the first thing he would say is, "How's your father?" That is priceless to me. So I worked for Court for a very long time.

A year later, I received a call from Scott D'Amore.

"David, would you be willing to come back to Impact and direct our shows again?"

"Of course I would. But just so you know, I am directing shows for MLW now."

"Oh, shit," D'Amore said. "I knew I should have called you sooner."

"Scott, it's okay. I never signed a no-compete clause with MLW, so I can direct both shows as long as there are no conflicts with the show dates."

"Thank you!"

"How much are you offering per show day?"

"Eight hundred dollars."

"That's insulting."

"That's what we pay our technical director now, David."

"Scott, I am a TV director, not a TD. And Court Bauer pays me nearly three times what you are offering."

"Really?"

"Yes. I'd never lie to you."

Flustered, Scott finally spoke.

"Okay, I really need you. How much do you want?"

"Let me think about this overnight and I'll let you know tomorrow. And don't worry, it will be very fair for both sides."

I was thrilled. The company I worked for most in my entire career, the one I helped build, was desperate for me to come back. But I had some concerns. The first person I called was Gail Kim, a TNA Hall of Famer and dear friend.

I wanted to know what the current environment was like at Impact. When I was "furloughed" (or "fired") the creative team was a mess, the production crew disgruntled and the locker room toxic. It was as if not a single person wanted to be there, except to earn a paycheck. I did not want to jump back into that depressing world I'd left behind a year ago.

"Scott asked me to come back and direct the shows again," I told Gail.

"Are you serious?" she asked, relief evident in her voice.

"Yes I am."

"David, that's great! I am so excited!"

"Me too. But Gail, be honest with me. I don't want to jump back in, even part-time, if the mood is still dour and the creative team so disorganized. The politics were toxic, too, when I left."

"David, it's a totally different company now. I swear to you. Everything has changed. Scott has gotten rid of all the disgruntled workers. The locker room is so positive, so united and tight. Please don't hesitate. Give it a shot. You will really like the new vibe here. I promise."

"Really?"

"Yes! It's nothing like it was before. Please give it a try."

"Gail, because you said so, I will."

The next day I called D'Amore.

"Scott, I'll be fair with my counteroffer."

"How much do you want?"

"Let's just split the difference between your lowball offer and what Court Bauer pays me. I'll even write all the promos and cold opens for the monthly pay-per-view events as well."

"No one has ever written or produced those opening videos as well as you. So, deal."

And so I was about to begin another era of working with TNA / Impact Wrestling.

31

RETURN TO IMPACT

My return to Impact Wrestling came in the spring of 2019. As with MLW, the first venue was the Melrose Ballroom in Queens.

The night before, I'd received a call from Eric Tompkins, then a producer for Impact Wrestling under Kevin Sullivan's tutelage.

"Hey, where are you?" Tompkins asked.

"I just got back to my room."

"Come on down to the hotel bar. Have a drink with us." It was an hour before midnight.

"I don't know. I want to make a good impression tomorrow."

"Come on down. A bunch of people here want to welcome you back. Me included." So I went.

It was a wonderful experience. Old friends from production and talent were happy to see me, and a handful of new wrestlers welcomed me, too. I was humbled and honored. More importantly, I was happy.

"So great to have you back!" some said.

"I've heard about you and all you have done," others would say. "I am so glad to finally meet you."

The next day I said hello to some more old friends at Impact, as well as a few of the stars. There were many new faces, most I didn't recognize.

It was a huge talent turnover in just over a year. Everything felt different, yet at the same time all felt right.

One of the friendly faces was Cody Deaner. He had returned to Impact a year earlier and was eager to welcome me back.

"The atmosphere when I returned last year felt really great," Cody said, backing up what Gail Kim had told me a week earlier. "It felt like it was a growth mindset, a mindset of 'let's rebuild this.'" I liked hearing that.

Years later I would ask Cody what the talent thought of my first day back, considering that most of the roster was now unfamiliar to me.

> I got a sense that many of the younger talents didn't know who you were. However, some of the older talents who'd been in the business much longer knew exactly who you were and were excited to have you on the team again. I know I was.
>
> I remember asking some young talent if they knew who that guy was as I pointed to you. They'd say no. I'd say, that's David Sahadi. They'd again say they don't know who that is, but the name sounds familiar.
>
> I'd then name all of the amazing Attitude Era moments that you helped create and brought to life over the years. Their eyes would go wide realizing that David Sahadi was the man behind the camera helping create the moments that made them want to become a professional wrestler.
>
> "That's the guy?" they asked me.
>
> "Yup, *that's* the guy."

The day I returned I indeed realized that a lot of the new talent knew nothing about me. I was the new guy, so once again I'd have to prove myself. I wasn't worried. Throughout my career I've done that many times.

After walking around the venue and introducing myself to the camera operators and crew, I went to the locker room. Again, most didn't know who I was, but I was greeted by Eddie Edwards, the locker room leader and a good friend whom I'd worked with before.

"Sahadi!" Edwards said with glee as he gave me a huge hug. "So good to have you back."

Publicity photo for a new wrestling show *KAYfABE* headed by Gail Kim and Christy Hemme.

BELOW: I don't think Bobby Lashley is impressed.

Andrew Thomas, once a TNA production assistant and now the lead truck producer for AEW.

Paying homage to my father as he recovers from a major brain trauma.

ABOVE: Laying the "SmackDown" on The Rock!

A little fun time with Velvet Sky at Universal Studios in Orlando.

Outside Soundstage 21 with my favorite tag team of all time, the Hardy Boyz.

A PR shoot for my first book, *My Dad, My Dying Sun*, a real-life story of love and legends, father and son.

A moment of reflection during the interview for my book, *My Dad, My Dying Sun*.

"The Charismatic Enigma" Jeff Hardy and TNA music producer Dale Oliver.

Velvet Sky in the hair and makeup room at Universal Studios.

BELOW: Directing a show for MLW in 2019.

The day before RAF01 and Poppa Lou is with me in spirit.

Chatting with Eric Bischoff and Jon Norton on the set of RAF01.

Working with Chris Chambers on a warehouse shoot with The Undertaker.

"Great to be back, Eddie," I replied. "I've missed you!"

That broke the ice for all those who didn't know me. Getting recognition from this leader and superstar brought validation.

"I was pumped when I saw him," Eddie would later say. "I got to know Dave during my time and always appreciated what he brought to our team. When you sit down and talk to Sahadi you can sense the love and passion he has for what he does. You can see it in the product. I'm proud to say that me and Dave have become really good friends over the years."

After leaving the locker room I proceeded to quietly walk around the ringside area. Many wrestlers were going through their matches, trying to decide the best places to do certain stunts and moves.

"I think the best place to do that move would be over here," I said to a couple of wrestlers I didn't know.

"Who are you?" they asked.

"I am the director of tonight's show."

"Why do you think that area is best?"

"Because it will be seen on four cameras, not just one," I replied, pointing to the cameras around the venue.

"Okay, thank you. We will do it there."

The first night went better than I'd ever dreamed. Andrew Thomas, the show's producer and a great friend ever since I joined TNA in 2004, made sure of that.

The next day, wrestlers came up to me.

"Hey, you captured that spot great!" one said.

"And I loved the way you cut the matches," said another.

"My entrance looked awesome! Thank you."

"Thank you guys for trusting me," I said.

"Are you really the guy Cody told us about?"

"I'm not sure what Cody said," I replied. "I'm just me."

All day long the wrestlers would approach me and ask where they should do certain spots and how I'd shoot their entrances. Being humble, I had gained their trust in a single day.

At this point in my career, I didn't need to be The Guy. I was just happy to be working with Impact Wrestling once again, knowing I could help make the product great again as well.

Later that night, when the show was over and the production crew was packing things up, I asked Eddie a question.

"Why did you stay during the dark times?"

"I think it's safe to say I am a pretty loyal person," Eddie replied. "Since day one TNA has always treated me very fairly. No matter who was in charge, they always treated me with respect. I also always felt very strongly that our locker room was one of the best around.

"We all had the same goal — to go further than we ever have been."

From this night onward, we were ready to go further than ever once again.

32

THE MASS EXODUS

It was a quintessential fall day in the southern United States. Comfortably warm, cloudless skies, and the excitement of NFL football about to fill the air.

My head, however, was in a state of a murky malaise. Admittedly, I was hungover. I had been off for a week and didn't have a show to direct for another six days. Then my phone rang. It was Scott D'Amore.

For a brief moment I pondered whether I should answer or wait an hour before calling him back, hoping some coffee would clear my head. After the fourth ring, before the call would go to voicemail, I decided to answer. I knew if Scott was calling on a Sunday, it must be for an important reason.

"Hello Scott," I said, trying my best to conceal my tired, hoarse voice.

"Hello David. Where are you now?"

"On my couch at home in Chattanooga."

"Can you come to Nashville this week?" There was urgency in his voice.

"Of course. Why?"

"Kevin Sullivan just quit and gave us five days' notice. And he is taking our entire postproduction team with him. The only person who made a stand and decided to stay is Eric Tompkins."

Tompkins was a very talented producer and Sullivan's right-hand man at the time. Every video package produced during those years was conceived, written and edited by Tompkins.

"You're joking, right?"

"I'm dead serious. Ed Nordholm is flying to Nashville as well. We need you this week."

"I'll be there."

I was stunned at first. Then pissed, for many reasons. The main one was that I knew what it meant. Without a production team in place, I'd have to return to Nashville on a regular basis to assist in production and would no longer be an independent contractor, free to direct shows for Impact, MLW, boxing and whatever else may come my way.

Second, I thought it was a betrayal on Sullivan's part. What kind of person negotiates with a competitor behind his own company's back and then gives his employer less than a week's notice and takes nearly the entire team with him to work for the competition — a team that knew all the ins and outs, all the secrets and mechanizations of Impact Wrestling?

Third, I still did not want to work in Nashville full-time again, and I had a sense this is where things were heading because of Sullivan's departure.

Damn Kevin Sullivan, I thought. His greed and ambitions were now going to take my freedoms and independence away. Of course the decision on going back to Nashville would ultimately be mine, and although I still wanted my flexibility, I did not want to abandon the company I loved when they needed me most.

Later that day, I called Eric.

"Hey Eric," I said, "I just heard the shocking news."

"It wasn't shocking for me," Tompkins replied. "I anticipated this would eventually happen and I've been planning for this day for a long time."

"I'm still shocked."

"Are you coming to Nashville?"

"Yes."

"Good. I'm sure Scott told you Ed is flying in from Toronto and I'd love to run some ideas by you."

One other person who didn't leave Impact at that time was Kenny Smith. Not by choice; Sullivan never gave him one. Sullivan thought Kenny was not worth paying big bucks to, and he was never more wrong.

Kenny has become one of the most talented and all-time best producers and editors in the business. And he wears many hats. He is an integral person in the television truck on live shows, perhaps even the team's MVP — double-checking every graphic each show, loading everything we need including video packages and backstage pre-tapes, and even working the EVS machine to record and prepare replays of high spots for us to roll into the shows. As an assistant producer / director / quality control coordinator and the replay producer during the frenzy of a live show, Smith kept me honest on everything: when lenses were dirty or cameras were slightly out of focus, and which shots to avoid because empty seats may appear. Smith was essential to my success on these productions.

Andrew Thomas was also someone I wanted to stay. Since my part-time return as an independent contractor in 2018, Thomas, once a production assistant and referee, had been my producer in the TV truck whenever I directed our shows. He was incredibly talented and always had a great attitude. Everyone loved Andrew. Back in June, Thomas was transparent and informed D'Amore he was being courted by All Elite Wrestling, and he was torn about what to do. Thomas was a TNA loyalist, but the offers from AEW were very enticing.

Later that Sunday night, I called Andrew from Chattanooga.

"Andrew, I hear you have an offer from AEW?"

"Yes I do."

"What are you going to do?"

"I'm still not sure. AEW is offering me a lot of money, and a chance to produce or direct the shows one day, and I'm leaning that way. It's tough, though, because TNA has always been my home."

"It *is* your home," I said, tugging at his heartstrings, "and you have ascended so fast in your career. Think about it. You started as a referee and have replaced legendary producer Keith Mitchell in the truck. I'm proud of you."

"Thank you."

"I love working with you, too. We make a great team."

"Yes we do."

"Do you really want to travel every single week?" I asked, still trying to speak to his heart, not his head. "Of all the production staff members that are leaving, you are the one I most want to stay and the one I am fighting hardest for. Ed Nordholm is coming to the Nashville studios this week to address the staff and to give you — and only you — a counteroffer. It's very fair. He doesn't give a damn about the others right now. He feels betrayed. Really, he is coming just to speak with you."

"That's good to hear," Thomas replied. "The decision is stressing me out."

"Please consider staying. Who knows if AEW will succeed in the long term?"

"After talking to you, now I am leaning that way. I really want to stay."

"I know you do. I'm coming to Nashville tomorrow afternoon. We can talk in more detail then."

Later that night, I received a call from Ed Nordholm.

"I'm flying to Nashville tomorrow evening," he told me. "I plan to go to the television studios and meet with Andrew the following day. Scott said you will be there, too."

"Yes I will."

"Good. And you say Andrew is the one worth trying to convince to stay, correct?"

"Absolutely. He is a fantastic producer and truly cares. And Eric Tompkins already has a plan for how to replace all those who are leaving."

On Monday evening, Ed, Eric and I had dinner to discuss the sudden changes, Eric's view for the future, and the value of Andrew staying on as a producer. We were convinced he would stay. The next morning, however, that belief was shattered. Somehow, Keith Mitchell had gotten wind of the fact we were giving Andrew a substantial raise to keep him, so Mitchell countered by increasing his offer from AEW. I was saddened. As talented and valuable as Andrew Thomas was, it was an offer not worth attempting to match.

I quickly relayed the news to Ed.

"This morning I heard that AEW increased their offer to get Andrew to jump ship," I told him.

"Is it essential that I try my best to keep him?"

"Not at all," Eric immediately replied. "He can be replaced. I have a backup plan for that as well."

"Good," Nordholm said. "Now I don't have to get on my knees to beg him to stay."

Andrew had no idea. He was expecting a counter. Nordholm knew he had the power now and played it masterfully.

First, Nordholm immediately made his presence known to the entire Impact Wrestling postproduction staff that would soon be leaving. He was cordial and smiling, but his message was more like, "So you think you screwed Impact, but what you don't know is we already have a team ready to replace you." Then he told Andrew they would speak soon.

Nordholm strategically kept Thomas waiting for nearly three hours.

"Are you doing okay?" I asked Andrew in edit room one.

"No. The wait is killing me."

"Don't let it. Just be yourself and hear him out."

"It's hard."

"I know, but remember you have two choices, and both are better than anything you ever had before."

"Thanks, Sahadi. I feel better."

I truly liked Andrew, both as a friend and a co-worker, and still do. Deep down I still held hope that a miracle would occur and persuade him to stay, but Mitchell's latest offer was too enticing. It all but sealed his fate at Impact Wrestling, and Nordholm would not be played.

Eventually, Thomas was summoned to the conference room at Skyway Studios to talk to Nordholm.

"So Andrew," Ed began, "I hear AEW is giving you a great opportunity. Tell me about it."

Thomas spent five minutes explaining the offer, the salary he would be paid and the responsibilities he'd have. Then he spent another few minutes describing all the skills he brought to Impact. Nordholm never interrupted, never said a word. When Thomas was done, he expected a counter from Nordholm. To his dismay, none came.

"I'm not even going to give you an offer to stay here," Nordholm said. "I am thinking about your future and I think this is a great opportunity for you and your family. If AEW becomes successful, I don't want you looking back with regret one day and saying, 'I wish I didn't stay at Impact.' So go to AEW, and I wish you well."

Well played, Ed.

When Andrew returned to the edit room, he was sullen.

"How did it go?" I asked.

"He didn't even make a pitch to keep me here," he replied, stunned and disappointed.

"He didn't give you an offer?"

"No. He just listened and then wished me well."

"I hate to see you go, I really do. I tried my best to keep you here."

"I know, Sahadi. You are a great friend."

"Well, I wish you well my friend."

Later that day, Eric Tompkins drove Ed and me downtown to meet for a drink with a superb audio engineer, Jay Seeman. Seeman had worked at TNA before and was truly talented. Ed had convinced him to rejoin. By the time the week was over, Tompkins had already created a new staff that would start on Monday: a senior producer for Impact, two editors to produce promos and video packages, an audio engineer and a production assistant. Plus we still had soon-to-be editor extraordinaire Kenny Smith, who within months would assume the role of senior producer for Impact Wrestling. I was amazed at Tompkins's determination and tenacity. He'd put together a full team in just days.

And soon more would join.

At this point, I was not a salaried employee for Impact or Anthem Sports & Entertainment. I was an independent contractor, paid a certain sum for each day I directed Impact's live events and TV tapings. D'Amore had promised me an exclusive contract in the future, and that wouldn't happen until November. Yet I wanted Eric to succeed, so I spent many days a week in Nashville helping produce the taped shows with Impact's new show editor. And I also worked with Tompkins on special stylistic shoots and cold open videos for our major pay-per-view events.

Over the next few months of working with Eric on these projects, I realized for the first time how incredibly creative he was. He was a visionary with a brilliant mind, and his rare talents would only continue emerging and expanding over the next few years. From a creativity standpoint, Eric was way ahead of Sullivan. His inventiveness reminded me of myself when I worked at WWE and when I first joined TNA.

For two decades I have been called a creative genius by those in the television industry, a pioneer who reinvented the way packages and show opens were written, filmed, edited and produced. No one else, they said, was on my level.

I'd finally found a creative peer, a visionary who was as talented and innovative as I felt I was. And in just a few years, Eric Tompkins would surpass me. He is the most creative person in wrestling production today.

33

THE FORBIDDEN DOOR OPENS

Don Callis called me just moments after I heard the big news.

"Can I ask a favor?" he said.

"Of course."

"Can you get your billionaire friend, Uncle Joe, to let us use one of his exotic RVs for a special shoot next week?"

"I can't promise but I will ask."

"Tremendous."

The special shoot was for Kenny Omega, an AEW megastar, and this was about to be a historic moment that would upend the wrestling world. Eric Tompkins had informed me minutes before Don called.

"Don't tell anyone," Callis demanded.

"I won't."

Eric had vowed silence, too, but he and I had discussed it thirty minutes earlier. We had to. This would be huge. And we needed each other to pull it off.

On December 2, 2020, on *AEW Dynamite*, Kenny Omega — with the help of Don Callis — turned heel and defeated Jon Moxley, capturing the AEW World Championship for the first time in front of a worldwide television audience. Then Omega and Callis rushed out of the ring and into the entrance tunnel, through the backstage where crew members were booing, and into a waiting limousine.

"They're running like scalded dogs," Jim Ross, the AEW announcer, said in disgust. "Callis, what a no-good bastard."

"Guys, guys, what did you just do?" asked backstage reporter Alex Marvez as they were entering the limousine. "What's going on here?"

"You'll find out this Tuesday night," Callis replied.

"Tuesday? *Dynamite*'s on Wednesday."

"This Tuesday night, on *Impact Wrestling* on AXS-TV, we will tell you what it's all about."

"We've been jobbed," Ross lamented as they went off the air.

Wow. This felt so real, so unscripted, even though Eric and I knew. It was executed so well that it reminded me of the Monday Night Wars in the late nineties.

The following Tuesday on *Impact Wrestling*, "The Belt Collector" Kenny Omega would make his intentions clear. Also known as "The Best Bout Machine," Omega declared he was at Impact for a single reason: to capture the promotion's World Championship so that he could add our title to his collection. And it became obvious to all that AEW and Impact Wrestling now had a working relationship, one never before seen in professional wrestling.

One month later at "Hard to Kill" in January 2021, Omega performed inside an Impact ring for the first time, teaming with "Bullet Club" in a six-man tag, and scored the pinfall.

Three months later at "Rebellion," The Belt Collector faced our reigning champion, Rich Swann, for the Impact World Championship. Of course he won the match, adding the Impact belt to his collection.

AEW's sole purpose was to portray Omega as the greatest wrestler in the world — but Omega's title run would last less than six months. AEW owner Tony Khan didn't want Omega to lose the title to what he perceived as a less-talented Impact opponent, especially on an Impact Wrestling show. Instead, on the premiere episode of *AEW Rampage* on August 13, 2021, Omega lost the Impact World Championship to AEW's own Christian Cage, once a member of TNA.

Personally, I thought that was beyond disrespectful. At that moment I knew the partnership between AEW and Impact was rapidly deteriorating.

For several months we had been overly accommodating to AEW. As part of the partnership, we even gave them a one-minute weekly infomercial in our shows to promote *AEW Dynamite*. It was hosted by Tony Khan and Tony Schiavone. Soon that one minute became two minutes, then four. The Tony and Tony show was taking advantage of our benevolence. What pricks.

What was really reprehensible to me was Tony Schiavone's lack of respect for our brand of wrestling, which — unlike AEW's — had great storylines, great video packages and talent vignettes, and emotional openings to our major shows. And although our stars were not as famous as theirs, ours were better athletes, and they put their hearts and souls into every single match they worked. Yet Schiavone would constantly mock Impact in these infomercials, spots that aired to our fans during our very own television program, making comments that were arrogant and disparaging. So disrespectful.

I have the utmost respect for Schiavone as a talent. Many consider him one of the best play-by-play announcers in wrestling history. I do not. He makes my Top 10 list, but not my Top 5. The person was far different from the mystique that fans admired.

I have two personal mottos. "If you mess with my father, you are messing with me" is one that I hold dear whenever someone attacks my beloved father, especially the way WWE did when they cut off his legends checks.

The second is, "If you don't respect me, fine. But then don't fucking expect me to respect you."

Schiavone never respected TNA/Impact. When I first met him, his contempt for the promotion was obvious. I never knew why. And he probably never even knew who I was or what I did, how I'd changed the landscape of professional wrestling two decades earlier, how in many ways I had a legacy equal to or greater than his.

As the relationship with AEW was deteriorating, we still had some "talent exchanges" from time to time. When AEW wanted to "borrow" the Good Brothers, they gave us Frankie Kazarian in return. And unlike their writers, or lack thereof, our finest wrote a great storyline. Frankie was returning to Impact Wrestling for one reason: a quest to fulfill something he never achieved while at TNA. Frankie was here to become the Impact World Champion for the very first time. It was a tremendous six-month story arc.

When I saw Frankie on his first day back, I sensed some trepidation. He was now a stranger in a world he'd been part of long before. Then I approached him.

"So good to see you, Frankie," I said with a smile.

"Great to see you, David."

"Frankie, this is not the same company you left. Everything is different. The locker room is the best I have ever seen. And everyone works with each other. Trust me, you will love your run here."

That seemed to comfort him. He had many great memories from TNA past, but dark moments from the chaos that was TNA when he departed still echoed in his memory. I was hoping he'd create some new memories at Impact Wrestling this time around.

"When I first returned to TNA," Kazarian would soon tell me, "I was still an active member of the AEW roster. It was surreal in a way. At first, I looked at it as closure.

"But the more I was around the locker room, and the talent and the crew, the more I became comfortable. It felt like home. It felt like a place where I belong. When I returned as a full-fledged member of the roster in January 2023, untethered to AEW, it felt to me like all was right in the world and this is where I needed to be."

It was where Frankie needed to be. His own heart told him so.

Overall, I think AEW got more out of the partnership than Impact Wrestling did. Cody Deaner agrees.

"I was excited about the opportunity of all the cross-promotional content that could be created," Deaner said. "I felt like there were endless possibilities for the fans to see some cool things they never thought they'd see.

"I was excited for Impact because as a 'company guy,' I've always just wanted to see Impact/TNA succeed. The more eyes on us the better. I've always thought we don't get the respect we deserve because not enough people see the amazing talent we have and the amazing product we put out."

Eddie Edwards also agrees.

"I think the idea of the 'Forbidden Door' was a good one," said Edwards, referring to a pay-per-view event produced by a similar partnership between rival promotions. "However the delivery was not. Without a doubt AEW got more out of that relationship than we did. We were treated like less-than."

Cody and Eddie said it all.

34

RIC FLAIR'S FINAL MATCH

It was an event for the ages. One that would captivate fans around the globe. One I thought I'd never be a part of.

Until less than two weeks beforehand.

After a production meeting on a Saturday morning in Louisville, Kentucky, I approached my boss, Scott D'Amore.

"Scott, I know Ric Flair's final match is in Nashville in two weeks," I said. "I love that guy and if you want me to assist in any way I will."

"David, two hours ago, before the production meeting, my answer would have been 'absolutely not.' But I just got off the phone with Conrad Thompson and I think his crew is in over their heads. Thank you for offering. I'll get back to you in a day or two."

"I will direct that show for free!"

Scott turned and looked me directly in the eye before saying with a smile, "Be careful what you wish for!"

What I wished for came true. I ended up having the honor of directing the four-hour pay-per-view, *and* it was for free. Didn't matter. It was a privilege to be able to say for the rest of my life that I was the one who directed "Ric Flair's Last Match."

The show was originally booked at the Nashville Fairgrounds, which held about 2,000 fans. It sold out in an hour, so it was moved to the

Nashville Municipal Coliseum, an arena with about 10,000 seats, and it was nearly a sellout there as well.

The most fascinating part of the show for me was the coming together of some of the world's greatest wrestlers, from nearly every promotion, to pay homage to a true legend, a self-proclaimed "wrestling god." Wrestlers from AEW, WWE, Impact Wrestling, Ring of Honor, Ohio Valley Wrestling, Major League Wrestling, Black Label Pro, Mexico's Lucha Libre AAA and New Japan Pro-Wrestling all participated.

What also impressed me was the passion of the production team. They were all fans of the "The Nature Boy" and were honored to be a part of this historic event. They understood its significance in wrestling history.

"When I was asked to be a part of the production for his last match, it was an automatic yes for me," said one of my camera operators, who goes by the name of Gator. "I was working for WWE at the time and didn't even ask for permission. I was doing it!"

"Finding out I'd be participating in the production for Ric Flair's Last Match was nothing short of exciting," said Kevin Martin, who operated a handheld camera for me. "In wrestling, you often lose sight of taking in the big moments because everything moves so quickly. Knowing we, the TNA production team, would be playing a major part in this historic night was a lot of fun."

As Erik Beaston wrote in the Bleacher Report, Flair's finale was "one more dance for the most respected in-ring competitor in professional wrestling, one more opportunity for the consensus best of all time to remind fans of his greatness and himself of the legacy he has compiled over the course of five decades in the industry."

The main event featured Ric Flair and his real-life son-in-law, Andrade El Idolo, against Jay Lethal and Jeff Jarrett. The match was not critically well received by the so-called wrestling experts online. Multiple reviews described watching Flair's performance in the main event as "uncomfortable" due to Flair's poor physical condition. The truth is, Flair was out drinking heavily the night before and was dehydrated. He got winded fast and even passed out twice during the match. The true heroes that night were Jarrett and Lethal, especially Jarrett and his wife Karen, who did a remarkable job of stalling, ad-libbing and taunting the rowdy crowd in an entertaining way to cover for Flair as he caught his breath. It was masterful.

Granted, it was not Ric Flair's best performance in a long, illustrious career. But did it matter?

Not at all. What mattered most was that the audience got the gift of witnessing the final match of this living legend's career, live and in person. They were there to pay tribute to one of their childhood heroes, a generational talent.

This was the first event to feature cooperation from all major American professional wrestling promotions since the 3rd Annual Brian Pillman Memorial in 2000, over two decades earlier. It was the second-highest-grossing independent pro wrestling event in history in North America, second only to "All In" in 2018, which was a precursor to the creation of AEW a year later.

Apart from the main event, the show was critically heralded as one of the best events of the year. The undercard matches were superb, exciting the entire crowd. The four-way match between Bandido, Laredo Kid, Rey Fenix and Black Taurus was the consensus pick for best match of the night. Dave Meltzer of the *Wrestling Observer Newsletter* gave it a rare 4.5 grade.

The production quality and overall presentation of the show was also praised. Funny thing was, the wrestling insiders who lauded the show's production values had no clue who produced this mega-event.

"What a great production," one said.

"The production team made the event look like a big-time WWE special," proclaimed another.

"Impact Wrestling should hire this production company to produce all of their shows," a third said. "It would make them look so much better."

What they didn't know was that it was Impact's own production team that produced the show, the very same team they criticized on a weekly basis. Funny how our excellent production engineers can make a show look more epic when we have nearly 9,000 fans in a big arena than when it's only several hundred in a nightclub or convention center.

"The relationship between a director and his camera crew can be an interesting dynamic," Gator said, "and can make or break a show. I had never worked with David Sahadi before, but it felt like we had worked together for years after only a match or two. Once we learned each other's rhythms, a trust was built, which is very important between a director and a camera operator. And I felt that professional connection and a TV kinship with David very early on.

"Just hearing 9,000-plus yell 'woooo!' and have tears come down their faces when Ric Flair stepped through the curtain was something I hadn't experienced in person until that day. Such raw energy. The chills were prevalent. To have played a small role in helping create such a massive moment was thrilling, and even saying that is an understatement."

Gator was right — it was an understatement. He was wrong about one thing, though. He played a huge role for me, not a small one.

Gator would reveal later that day that he was a fan of mine before he even knew my name:

> In college, my roommate and I ordered every PPV. The opening videos that WWE produced were mind-blowing to a young man looking to do high-quality work in the TV industry. The best in the television business. Every month, the new open topped the previous one. I didn't know it at the time, but all of my favorites were produced by David Sahadi. It took years to read about it in behind-the-scenes articles, but once I discovered that all my favorites were made by David, it put a goal in my mind: I have to make pro wrestling content with David Sahadi someday. And at Flair's Last Match, that happened.

What a great compliment. I was humbled.

When the event was over, I walked backstage to see everyone involved. The green room was exuberant and crowded, and I saw familiar faces from my past at WWE.

"David Sahadi," The Undertaker said, "so good to see you. What are you doing now?"

"Well, besides directing tonight's show, I am back at Impact Wrestling full-time."

"So happy to hear that. Miss those shoots we did together."

"Me too. You were always my favorite."

Bret "The Hitman" Hart greeted me next, and then Mick Foley. We talked fondly of our time building an empire in the late nineties and early 2000s.

Then two young wrestlers approached me, still in their ring gear.

"Are you really *the* David Sahadi?" they asked.

"Yes."

"This is remarkable! We are here because of you tonight."

I was perplexed.

"How so?" I asked. "I had nothing to do with the writing or the booking of the show."

"You don't understand," one said. "When I was a kid, I saw your videos and packages you produced for WWE. They were awesome! They inspired me to become a professional wrestler. So because of your creative work, I am here tonight!"

"You gave us a purpose," the other said, "to become who we are today."

"Thank you," I said, a number of times.

I was overwhelmed by their kind words. That moment was an eye-opener, realizing my work had changed people's lives — kids I never knew, parents I would never meet. Hundreds of thousands of people, maybe millions, too. The moment both mystified and enlightened me at the same time.

Yes, I directed Ric Flair's Last Match for free. But I was also paid handsomely — not with a paycheck, but an abundance of spiritual currency when I discovered the impact I had made on so many people's lives.

What greater gift is there than that?

35

TALES FROM THE TRUCK

"The house is on fire!"

One thing about being the director of a live wrestling show is that one must always expect the unexpected. Despite the scripts and formats, the unexpected always happens, in ways big and small. And sometimes in ways never imaginable.

One such time was in the summer of 2006 when a fire broke out inside Soundstage 21 at Universal Orlando — just as we went on air with our first match.

Wrestling fans have always loved a great pyrotechnics display to open a show. Flames, fireballs and dramatic explosions always get the crowd — and the viewer — fired up. But it was all too literal this time.

It was the opening of TNA's "Hard Justice" pay-per-view, and the sparks from the opening pyro unexpectedly set a sack bag in the upper rafters on fire. As the first match started, smoke started to fill the studio. Crew members raced up flights of rafters to extinguish the flames, but the chemicals they used only made the smoke worse. A minute later, a cloud of smoke descended upon the ring. The match could not be seen, except for brief glimpses from handheld cameras at ringside.

Minutes later fire marshals stopped the match and the studio was evacuated. Fans, talent and crew included. We were live on a worldwide pay-per-view. What would we do?

Jeff Jarrett quickly pivoted. He directed us to cut to spontaneous live interviews with the TNA wrestlers outside the studio while I kept an unmanned, locked-down camera shooting the smoke and firefighters inside, and we cut back and forth. We were stalling, but it was spontaneous and real, and because of that it was compelling.

"When Soundstage 21 caught fire," Frankie Kazarian recalled, "I was on deck as I was involved in the next match. They evacuated the buildings, and everybody was kind of in a holding pattern."

The fire marshals wanted us to cancel the show. Jeff Jarrett pleaded with them for forty-five minutes, and with his great powers of persuasion convinced the fire marshals to let the crowd back inside. The show continued and we were able to get most of the matches on the air, except one.

"Ultimately, my match was the only one that got cut that evening," Frankie said.

Jeff Hardy / Victory Road 2011

Another surreal time directing a live show occurred at Victory Road in Orlando in 2011.

It was minutes before the live main event, and I had to talk to D-Lo Brown, the agent for the world championship match, through my headset while I had the chance.

"D-Lo?"

Silence. A taped video package was winding down and soon we would be back live in the Impact Zone.

"D-Lo, can you hear me?"

Crickets. It was only with twenty seconds remaining that I finally heard a voice.

"Give me a minute Sahadi," D-Lo said. "I'm working with a talent who may not be able to make it to the ring right now."

That talent was Jeff Hardy, and in this match he was set to battle "The Icon" Sting for the TNA World Heavyweight Championship. The plan was for Hardy to win the title. Although Hardy had seemed fine when I'd last seen him before the show, he was suddenly incapable of performing in a safe and professional way.

We stalled for reasons I did not know at the time. I was in the television production truck parked just outside Soundstage 21, and D-Lo was in the arena at the "go" position just behind the curtains, where the wrestlers would make their entrances to a worldwide TV audience and the live crowd.

"OK, we are good to go," D-Lo told me seconds later. "I'll talk you through this as it happens. This has the potential to be a train wreck."

Jeff Hardy's music then played, and it took a long time before he emerged from the smoke in the tunnel. Forty-five seconds to be exact. It was awkward. I kept taking shots of the overhead jib camera to buy some time, interspersed with shots of a cheering crowd as well as the stage. When Hardy finally did appear it was obvious he was under the influence of something. He wobbled down the entrance ramp and even slipped trying to go up the steel stairs and enter the ring.

Then Sting's music played, and he walked to the ring with a purpose. He was obviously upset. They stared each other down in the center of the ring, and before the bell rang, Eric Bischoff's music played, and now here he was striding to the ring with resolve as well. None of this was scripted or planned. They were ad-libbing, and I had no clue what was about to happen.

Eric cut a promo before going to each wrestler to whisper something in their ears. To his credit, he gestured with his hands to make it seem like he was talking smack to the other combatants. In reality, Bischoff was giving them instructions on how the match needed to play out with Hardy now inebriated. He was buying time while also trying to add some intrigue for the audience. I am not sure Hardy actually understood what Bischoff was telling him.

This match would now be a No Disqualification match, a smart decision the creative team made on the fly. This was done to protect the performers and prevent a disaster from happening if Jeff Hardy did something stupid or used a weapon. It was damage control, protecting

Hardy from hurting himself or Sting if he tried a dangerous move, one he was incapable of doing in his current state.

Before the match started, referee Brian Hebner even put up the dreaded "X" sign indicating Jeff was in no state to compete, but the match went on anyway.

The bell rang and the match instantly stalled. Instead of locking up or going right into combat, Jeff Hardy teased over and over again that he would throw his T-shirt into the crowd. Sting didn't move, instead staring at Hardy with piercing eyes. He looked rightfully pissed. This moment went on way too long.

The fans finally saw some action as Sting slowly and methodically backed Jeff into a corner. Sting hit Jeff a few times, then suddenly put him into a scorpion death drop. Jeff attempted a kick-out at the end of the second count, but Sting held firm for the pin. Just like that the match was over, in a mere two minutes. Like a disappointed father, Sting then stared a hole into Jeff, who slowly and unsteadily got up, confused after the pinfall and generally bewildered by what was going on. Hardy was supposed to win this match, and with it the TNA World Heavyweight Championship.

As a furious Sting walked up the ramp, a fan yelled, "That was bullshit!" Sting acknowledged him.

"I agree," Sting replied. "Yes, it was."

Scott Steiner's Heart Attack

In March 2020, just before COVID shut the world down, we taped a special show called "TNA Homecoming" at the Coca-Cola Roxy nightclub in Atlanta.

I invited my good friend Jonathan Gordon, a die-hard wrestling fan, to attend. It was a dream come true. He was handed a backstage pass, which gave him access to anywhere he wanted to go.

The show was written to pay homage to the great stars of TNA past. It was nostalgia mixed with great matches. We even had the legendary voice of Barry Scott, the first voice-over announcer I ever used when I joined TNA in 2004, to do the narration for the promos, the cold open and even the bumpers within the show. Little did I know it would be the night Scott Steiner suffered a severe heart attack backstage.

Jonathan was a quiet witness when it occurred. I was in the truck directing the show and had no idea. Here is how Jonathan described what he saw:

> I had the incredible opportunity to attend a live Impact wrestling match featuring the legendary professional wrestler Scott Steiner as a special guest. From the moment I stepped backstage, I was enveloped in the electrifying atmosphere of the event. The scents of sweat, pyrotechnics, leather, cleaning products, and a full food/beverage concession stand filled the air. Despite my nerves, I actually could contain my excitement as I caught glimpses of my favorite wrestlers preparing for their matches backstage. But nothing could prepare me for the awe-inspiring sight of Scott Steiner walking out with his chainmail, exuding an aura of strength and power reminiscent of a medieval warrior.
>
> After his match, as Scott returned to the lunch hall, a sudden hush fell over the bustling backstage area. I had no clue what happened to him between the time he left the stage to the time he sat down in the lunch area. I barely peered inside to witness a distressing scene — Scott Steiner, the wrestling icon I admired, was on the ground, surrounded by concerned onlookers.
>
> The air grew thick with tension as everyone gathered around him, their expressions reflecting fear and worry. In a touching display of solidarity, everyone in the room took a knee, a silent tribute to their fallen comrade . . . Without exchanging a word, we instinctively joined together in a silent prayer for Scott Steiner's well-being. Each of us, whether fans, wrestlers, or staff, bowed our heads in reverence, sending our thoughts and hopes for his recovery. It was a small gesture, but one filled with immense significance — a testament to the profound impact Scott had on the wrestling

> community and the genuine care we all felt for him in that moment of crisis . . .
>
> The urgency of the situation was underscored by the swift arrival of an ambulance, its siren piercing through the quiet atmosphere. Paramedics sprang into action, administering CPR and carefully loading Scott onto a stretcher. As I stood in the hallway, the weight of the moment sank in. It felt eerily reminiscent of the tense atmosphere when Damar Hamlin went down for the Buffalo Bills, both instances highlighting the harsh realities of competitive sports . . .
>
> Hours later, relief washed over me as news spread that he was stable and alive, albeit having suffered a heart attack. Though shaken by the ordeal, I felt grateful that one of my wrestling heroes would pull through.

I had no idea. I first heard the news after the show in a bar across the street. Jonathan found me.

"Scott Steiner had a heart attack tonight," he said.

"Stop fucking with me, Jonathan."

"No really, he did."

I knew he was serious now.

"Is he okay?"

"They took him to the hospital. I hope he survives."

We both kneeled on the wooden floor, held hands and said a prayer.

The Atlanta No-Show Event

In the summer of 2022, we had a live three-hour event at Center Stage in midtown Atlanta, "Against All Odds." The name could not have been more fitting for what was to unfold that day.

We had our small Nashville production team present and had booked twenty local freelancers to work as camera operators, audio technicians, grips, and gaffers, as well as handle other aspects of a live television broadcast, including setup and breakdown.

Then a funny thing happened. On the day of our show, our technical manager, the man in charge of booking the crew, never showed up. Neither did eighteen of the twenty freelancers. We were perplexed at first. Calls to the tech manager went directly to voicemail. So did calls to the missing crew. Texts sent were never replied to.

Something was definitely not right.

Then panic set in. There were still seven hours before showtime, and we were looking for replacements to staff the production team. Friends called other production friends that lived near Atlanta. All were busy or booked for other events out of town. The director of production posted a notice on Facebook asking if anyone near Atlanta was available. Two people responded, and only one, a handheld-camera operator, showed up.

"When I was first told about the majority of the production crew no-showing, we had just arrived at the venue," recalled Kevin Martin, a shooter/editor for Impact. "Originally, we thought it was a joke to try and have some fun ahead of how busy things were going to be that day. However, it soon became apparent that this was not a joke, and now we were asking the question, 'What now?'"

I, however, was not stressed.

"It's going to be a glorious day," I kept telling the frenzied crew, a line I borrowed from a song by Radiohead.

"Why aren't you stressed?"

"Because I can't control who shows up and who does not. That's up to you guys."

"It's going to be a disaster."

"No, it's not," I insisted. "Just get me two camera ops and I'll direct a decent show. Get me four camera ops and I'll direct a great show."

"We need six or eight."

"I'd like six or eight, but I'll settle for two."

"Really?"

"Yes. 'It's gonna be a glorious day.'"

They couldn't understand my lack of stress, but if I can't control something I just make the best of the situation.

My call time was 12 noon. Bryan Roof, nicknamed "Cornbred," was our sole regular ringside camera operator who traveled to our events on the road. I also let him be the "floor director" of all the handhelds, a title that doesn't really exist but one he was enamored with. Roof's talents are amazing, and he's a great teacher to other camera operators as well. Roof was at the arena six hours beforehand and knew more than I knew. This is his recollection of the events that morning:

> Atlanta was my first real traveling show with Impact. Before that, I had driven my own vehicle to Cincinnati and Nashville, and I slept on the spare bed in the tech manager's hotel room. This time, I rode down with two other guys from Louisville and I was going to have to pay for my own room. It was all a part of paying dues to earn a spot, and I was prepared to show how bad I wanted to travel with Impact.
>
> The night before, I saw Dave Sahadi down in the lobby and his face lit up when he saw me. He gave me a big hug and said, "Cornbred! You made it!"
>
> The following morning, I showed up at Center Stage at 8 a.m. I was the only person there except for the truck engineers. We waited and waited for the rest of the crew to show up. Nobody ever came. I called the tech manager to ask what was going on, and he never answered.
>
> I had only set the show up a few times and didn't really know how it all went together. But I knew that things had to be done before we went live on pay-per-view that evening. I worked with the engineers to run camera cables and feeds into the arena, hoping that the rest of the crew was just late, or lost, or trying to find a parking spot. After we assembled the "hard" cameras we realized we were pretty much done with setup. Covered in sweat, aching backs, and still no crew.
>
> Just a few hours until showtime and the people hired as replacements for the original crew started trickling in. They grabbed one of the lighting guys and had him work one of the hard cameras. I had to recruit some of the local wrestling talent to sit low in the vomitory stairwells and wrangle our camera cables during the show so we wouldn't

> get tangled and trip. Dave Sahadi came in to survey the arena and get his vision together, because he can only see so much from the truck. He paused for a moment, looked around, and said, "Hey, where's the jib?"
>
> The jib camera is a camera on the end of a long beam that is able to float over the crowd and around the ring. We typically use the jib shots at the beginning of every match segment so we can establish where we are and show the whole arena in a different, creative way. We didn't have a jib camera or anyone to run it even if we did!
>
> I told Dave that he could always just take my camera shot and I could move it creatively to accomplish the same thing. I don't remember who coined the term, but we ended up calling these types of shots "Corn-Jib" shots!

Kevin Martin was the second-most-important handheld-camera operator, shooting opposite Cornbred. Even though it was his first time shooting live for me, I had faith in Kevin.

"Being thrust into a ringside cameraman role was exciting for me, oddly enough," Kevin recalled. "This was my first time shooting ringside for Impact/TNA, and I felt this was an opportunity for not only myself but our entire postproduction team to pull off a massive feat and show our worth in a whole different way. I felt pretty confident about our abilities, and our goal now was to knock this out of the park as best as we could with the resources available."

Cornbred said, "I think we put on a heck of a show from top to bottom that night. I don't suspect anyone in the live audience or watching at home would say any different. It's something I am personally proud of, as should the rest of our team. It never got out that the production crew didn't show up, so there were no expectations of it going downhill or anything like that. But *we* knew what was going on, and being able to live up to our standard with a *very* skeleton crew was a testament to how hard-working this team is."

"To me, it was just another show," Bryan Roof added. "Load it in, shoot the show, load it out. Make it happen. But to everyone who was there, that's the weekend I proved myself, and I've been traveling with Impact/TNA ever since."

And as Martin summed things up, "This night was one for the memories and I feel like this was proof that this team will keep moving forward no matter the circumstances."

It turned out to be one of our greatest shows ever. We had four camera operators, two of them Roof and Martin. As for the two hard cameras, one was operated by a freelance audio engineer we pulled from working on backstage pre-tapes, and the other was the sole operator who answered the call. We also had a great A1, responsible for mixing the live show. He was the only crew member that was booked that did show up.

We were a motley crew for sure, but what made the show so wonderful was the performance put on by the athletes inside the ring combined with the production team's commitment to doing whatever was necessary to help the show.

They were put in unfamiliar roles, but they were not timid. Heart and passion won out.

Yes, at Against All Odds, we pulled off something that was truly against all odds.

36

THE RETURN OF TNA

It was a plan over six months in the making, one never leaked by the few staff and production people who knew about it before the big reveal. That in itself was remarkable.

The announcement would be made at Impact Wrestling's biggest pay-per-view event of the year, Bound for Glory, on October 21, 2023. It was shocking and it was major: Impact was going back to its original name, the first time since 2017 that we would be known as TNA Wrestling.

The announcement came at the end of the event in an incredible, creative four-minute video produced by Eric Tompkins.

"I can still hear it," Frankie Kazarian says in the video to his fellow veterans of the first TNA. "People want to pretend that it went away, but we're reminded of it every fucking day.

"All of you, you're my brothers and my sisters. And I feel it in my core. Professional wrestling is bleeding. There needs to be a change. This is that change."

"And to get there, we have to go back to where it all started," Jordynne Grace added.

Eric Young, Alisha Edwards, Eddie Edwards, Alex Shelley, Josh Alexander and Chris Sabin also spoke in the video. It ended with a box being opened that revealed the return of TNA. This rebrand would go into effect starting with our first major pay-per-view of 2024, "Hard to Kill," at the Palms Casino Resort in Las Vegas on Saturday, January 13.

Fans were ecstatic. Before there was AEW there was TNA, founded in 2002, for those disenchanted fans who wanted a different wrestling promotion to follow. Back then, TNA was that alternative.

"When Impact rebranded back to TNA, I for one was pretty psyched," Kazarian told me. "I was in the know months before most of the world found out, and I was an integral part of the shoot that announced to the world what was about to happen. It was honestly one of the most exciting times I've ever had in the company."

"We still hear the 'TNA' chants wherever we go," company president Scott D'Amore would say. "Fans have longed for TNA Wrestling, so that's what we're bringing back in 2024: TNA Wrestling, we're back!"

There would be a new set, a new logo, new championship belts and a new attitude.

"Part of any great company is looking back and celebrating your history and successes," D'Amore said. He wanted TNA to be proud of who they are instead of running away from the past.

"Impact Wrestling had a ton of momentum at the time, but it felt like there was something missing," said Eddie Edwards. "This was it. There was such a strong sense of positivity as soon as we announced we were rebranding back to TNA. And in the world of wrestling, that is very rare. The momentum hasn't stopped since."

In the immediate aftermath of TNA's revival, just after we'd wrapped shooting four weeks of shows in late January, a major bombshell would fall. On February 7, 2024, Anthem Sports & Entertainment announced that D'Amore's contract had been terminated, and he would be replaced by Anthony Cicione, Anthem's president of entertainment.

Everyone in TNA, from production to the talent roster, was shocked. This couldn't be happening. The news came out of nowhere, with no tremors beforehand to warn of the coming earthquake.

Scott D'Amore was the heart and soul of TNA Wrestling. Most of the talent on the current roster was there only because of him. Most of production, too, myself included. I had known Scott since the first day I arrived at TNA in the fall of 2004, and we immediately connected, like two long-separated brothers reuniting. Scott was more than a boss; he was a dear friend.

Later that night, my mind harkened back to a year earlier. My beloved father had been dealing with multiple health issues, and Scott had allowed me to stay with my dad at his home in Boca Raton for the last three months of his life and just travel to direct the TV shows.

The morning I was planning to drive to Atlanta to direct a live pay-per-view, my dad was not doing well. His significant other, Susan, and I decided to take him to the emergency room.

When we arrived he was instantly given an IV. After an hour of tests, the ER doctors said it was simply severe dehydration, nothing more. With Susan by his side, I decided to begin the ten-hour drive to Atlanta.

So I left. But I hedged my bet.

I drove only to Savannah, Georgia, the midway point between the hospital and Atlanta, and got a room for the night. I put my phone on my chest as I went to bed, hoping an emergency call would not awaken me, but ready to return to the hospital if it did. Thankfully none came, but I barely slept. How could I?

Later that morning as I was driving to Atlanta, Susan called.

"They just found out he has pneumonia," she told me.

"I'm coming back now."

"No. Go to Atlanta. He's going to be okay."

"Are you sure?"

"Yes. The doctors said we got him to the hospital just in time. Had we waited even one more day, he would not be coming home. Go to Atlanta. I got this."

She really did.

I arrived in Atlanta just hours before the live pay-per-view broadcast, Hard to Kill. I chuckled at the irony. That was my dad in a nutshell.

The show was a success. It received critical acclaim from all the wrestling websites. On Saturday, I planned to direct two taped episodes of *Impact Wrestling* and then drive immediately back to Boca. Just a few hours before showtime, I approached my boss, D'Amore.

"Scott, do you mind if I let Kenny direct the last few matches of the second show?" Kenny Smith was my protégé.

"Let him direct the entire second show," Scott said. "Why do you ask?"

"My dad is in the hospital. He may be coming home early tomorrow. He has pneumonia and will be fine. I'm just still deeply concerned."

"Then leave right now!" Scott demanded.

"He's with his significant other. He's okay."

"Leave, and let Kenny direct both shows tonight. Be with your father."

"Let me just direct the first show. Then I'll leave."

"You are not directing either show," Scott insisted. "But if it will make you feel better, just stay in the production truck for the first match or two, then give Kenny a pat on the back and say 'you got this.'"

I stayed for six matches, not two. Before leaving I wanted to thank Scott. I found him at the "go" position, the master control section backstage, watching monitors and dictating orders through a wireless headset and microphone.

"Kenny's doing fine," I told him. "Thank you. I'm leaving now."

Scott looked at me in shock and annoyance as he removed his headset.

"What the fuck are you still doing here?" he said loudly. "You should have left hours ago! Go be with your father. Go now."

I drove straight through the night, with a few energy drinks to keep me awake and alert. He was released when I arrived and we brought him back that day.

That's the person Scott D'Amore is. He always put family above work, and that's why we were so surprised that he was fired. We weren't just losing a friend; we were losing a part of our family.

Two days later, on a Zoom call, Anthem Sports head Len Asper would explain the reasons for Scott's dismissal. Anthony Cicione was present as well and told everyone that he had an open-door policy and that this business decision had the future of TNA in mind. We were promised TNA would grow and reach new heights. Watching the reactions of the talent on the call, especially Josh Alexander, I could tell the news cut deep. Hearts were bleeding and futures were uncertain.

Days later, numerous TNA performers would write a letter to Anthem requesting D'Amore's return to TNA. I never saw the original letter, but here is a sample of what some wrestling insiders were told about its content:

> TNA/Impact is not just our employer and the company for which we work. It is a family. A family that each of us has

grown to love and cherish and trust with our bodies and our careers. A family for which we feel deeply and desire, above all else, to protect.

We are deeply saddened by the decision to remove Scott D'Amore from the TNA/Impact family. Scott is a brilliant wrestling mind that has guided this company and positioned it to take the next step upward in our industry. Scott is also so much more than this. He is a trusted friend, confidant, teacher, advisor, brother, and mentor to so many within the TNA/Impact family. Scott has been the heart of this family for over two decades . . .

We understand and appreciate that professional wrestling, at its core, is a business, and that the company must provide a fiscally responsible, financially viable product. At the same time, professional wrestling is uniquely situated. The business of professional wrestling is so much more than balance sheets, downloads and ratings. The wrestling business is and must be its people, its characters and its storylines . . . there is no wrestling business without creative vision and the right people bringing the creative vision to life.

It is our desire to have a dialogue with you and with the company in an effort to protect the present and the future of TNA/Impact for you, for Anthem, for the fans and for professional wrestlers. We feel strongly that a "wrestling person" needs to be intimately involved at a high level to ensure that the amazing company we have all built and product we have provided to our fans continues to grow and flourish. It is our opinion that the best possible person for that role was, is, and will be Scott . . .

We look forward to hearing from you and continuing this dialogue.

Signed, Your TNA Family.

Len Asper is an astute businessman with great acumen for reading the room. He sensed an impending revolt, so he took an unplanned flight to

New Orleans on February 3 to personally address the entire TNA roster. Asper was candid and straightforward, and what he had to say allayed most of the wrestlers' fears. I had a feeling, however, that not all were fully satisfied.

There would be aftershocks to come. The legendary Motor City Machine Guns, a tag team made up of Alex Shelley and Chris Sabin, would have their last match in Philadelphia at the end of March when their contracts expired. These renowned world champions were students of Scott D'Amore, and I think their passion for TNA vanished when Scott was dismissed.

Others would leave soon, though some returned and new faces joined. Wrestling, like life, is often a carousel ride.

No one likes change. It is human nature to resist anything that challenges our norms, our belief systems, our status quos. We like to remain nestled in our comfort zones.

But in order to grow, change is necessary. Change is how we adapt and reinvent ourselves, how we evolve, like how a caterpillar enters its cocoon and emerges a beautiful butterfly with wings to fly.

37

TERMINATED

The phone call came unexpectedly on a warm, sunny afternoon in late May. It was Anthony Cicione, who'd replaced Scott D'Amore as TNA president just a few months earlier.

"I have some bad news for you," he said. "Your employment with TNA has been terminated as of today."

I was too shocked to reply until the gravity of what he'd just said sank in.

"May I ask why?"

"We are restructuring. Thank you for the three months I knew you. Now I am going to transfer you to human resources."

And that was it.

So sudden, and so cold. After I'd worked nearly twenty straight years for TNA — through all the ups and downs, the changes of leadership, the many pay cuts — all this new president, this man who'd just terminated my employment, could offer me was a mere fifteen seconds of his time on a phone call. And even the transfer to human resources went to voicemail.

I was numb. How could this be? Just one day earlier, I was on our weekly production conference call with Anthony and the top executives of the company, and they were delighted to hear the creative changes I suggested to the *Impact!* show. Twenty-four hours later, I was terminated.

The term "restructuring" is a handy euphemism for cost-cutting. TNA Wrestling had been hemorrhaging money for over a year, so it became apparent they were eliminating the older employees with big contracts and promoting younger employees from within to cut costs. A savvy business decision, yes, but one devoid of heart, bereft of emotion and lacking even a modicum of empathy.

Then a funny thing happened. Within minutes, a feeling of relief engulfed me. To be totally honest, deep down there was a part of me that wanted this. A part of my heart died the day Scott D'Amore was fired. Scott and I have an enduring bond; we connected on my first day at Soundstage 21. Then he was a talent, "Coach D'Amore," and he smiled a lot. One year after I was furloughed in 2018, Scott called and asked me to return, and I didn't hesitate — I was on a flight two days later. And it was Scott's idea to change the name back to TNA. It was a brand, and something the fans yearned for. The chants of "TNA! TNA!" still echoed in the hearts of many, none more than Scott. He bled TNA red. He successfully brought the brand back, and got fired for it. How could they?

So I was relieved that I was no longer employed by TNA, no longer had to travel to Nashville on a weekly basis to help edit the show, no longer had to endure conference calls that were three times longer than they needed to be. And summer was almost here. I was financially secure, and now I had the entire season off. Perhaps I would take another cross-country trip by car, like the one twenty years earlier when I left WWE. That thought brought a smile to my face.

Later that day, I tried calling human resources again. This time a woman answered.

"Hello David," she said with polite trepidation. "I have heard nothing but good things about you, and I hate that our first conversation we ever have is about your termination."

She seemed genuinely upset, so I replied calmly and gently.

"Julie, it's okay. I lost my father one year ago, and I can never get him back. Today, I lost a job, but I can get another one tomorrow."

"You are so kind," she said, relief in her voice. "Everyone said you were one of the nicest people one could ever meet, and I hear the kindness in your voice."

"Kindness is a choice, Julie. Why would I be mad at you when you are merely the messenger?"

"Wow. It's been a long day and I'm so happy you are my last call because the others did not take the news very well and most of them screamed and cussed at me."

"Others?" I inquired, my curiosity piqued. "I'm not the only one?"

"No. There were about two dozen other calls, and no one took the news as well as you."

"I can't even imagine how tough that must have been for you." My empathy for her was genuine, but I also knew those words might later work to my benefit.

"Very tough. Thank you for being so kind. Now before I send over your severance package, I want to go over the details with you first."

"That's fine, but you know I have a contract, don't you?"

"A contract?" she asked, completely caught off guard. She had no idea. "Does Anthony know?"

"Apparently not, since he fired me so hastily."

"Do you have a copy of the contract you can send me?"

"No, I do not. I signed it five years ago and handed it right back to Scott."

She seemed befuddled. Apparently I was the only one who was cut that day that had an actual signed contract.

"What does it say?"

"The contract states that if I get fired through no fault of my own, I receive six months of pay. It also states that I receive a $25,000 bonus every year in the first week of April. That bonus check was due two months ago and never arrived."

Silence for a few moments.

"David," she eventually replied, "I am not going to send you your severance package now. You've been so polite, and I did not know you had a contract, so I want to do right by you. Give me a few days to see if I can find a copy of it somewhere. It's the least I can do."

"Take a couple of weeks if you need," I said. "I'm not in a rush."

It's a funny thing getting fired. You learn a lot about yourself. You also learn a lot about your friends, especially the employees you worked with in the trenches through all the days and nights that turned into dawn.

Only two people reached out to me that day, both via text. One was Eric Tompkins. The other was Ariel Shnerer, a vice president from Anthem Sports & Entertainment who, unlike Anthony, had a genuine heart and kind spirit and was at this time the true driving force at TNA, the glue that held everything together.

Two days later it was I who did the outreach. I got hold of Gail Kim, a friend who was then the head of talent relations for TNA.

What a wonderful conversation. Gail and I had a strong friendship that was nearly two decades in the making. She couldn't understand why I was terminated. Then I told her that my conversation with Anthony lasted only fifteen seconds.

"*What?!*" she screamed, as if suddenly awakened from a slumber by a loud noise. "He only talked to you for fifteen seconds?"

"Give or take a second or two."

"That motherfucker. I am so outraged. I am going to call him first thing on Monday and rip him a new asshole. I'm going to tell him what a huge fucking mistake he made. It's the worst mistake of his career. Not only are you so talented, but your energy is so positive. The entire locker room feeds off that. And he treated you like a nobody, after all you did."

Later that evening I called Kenny Smith, the show editor who'd just inherited my job, and congratulated him. For the last two years I had been training Kenny to become a director, knowing one day it would be his time to shine, and I was genuinely happy that it had come, albeit so suddenly. Kenny is one of the few good guys in the cruel world of sports entertainment, and I had a sense he was leery of reaching out to me because he felt awkward about how things transpired.

"David, I had no idea this was happening," Kenny said when I called him. "I feel so bad. I owe you everything."

"Kenny, you owe me nothing," I said. "You are so talented, and I am so proud of you. You deserve this. Now make me proud and have a killer show next weekend!"

Another interesting thing happened that weekend. Two days after my termination, I drove to Atlanta to say hello to Court Bauer at Major League Wrestling. I'd planned this trip months in advance when I saw that MLW had a show just ninety minutes away from where I live.

When I arrived, I had a brief talk with Court backstage just before the live show began. I didn't want to take up too much of his time in this moment. I knew better. As I drove home, I reflected on how seeing people I'd worked with during my earlier stint with MLW felt like coming home.

The following Monday, Court sent me a text. "So, what did you think?" We agreed to have a conversation on Thursday. But the very next day we agreed that I would rejoin MLW Wrestling as an executive producer. Though I'd wanted the summer off, I felt a desire, a need, to be there at this decisive moment in time. MLW had momentum on their side, and I wanted the opportunity to try and take it to another level.

I truly believe that within the heart of MLW Wrestling lies an amazing brand yearning to emerge and showcase its immense potential. "If only" is MLW's only barrier: if only we had a better TV deal, if only we had a live streaming deal on a larger platform, if only our budget wasn't so limited.

What made up for the limitations, however, was the limitless passion and care of all who worked there. When people are passionate and dream big, those dreams eventually become reality. What a glorious day that will be for all who believed and worked relentlessly without ever asking "why?"

MLW had sold out every show for over a year, an incredible feat that neither WWE nor AEW could claim. The fan experience was tremendous, and I wanted the opportunity to try and capture that on the television side.

After directing my first show for MLW in July, I asked Court if I could help in postproduction. That has always been my forte. Court was happy I wanted to take on more and allowed me to work directly with some of the editors in the creation of their packages, promos and graphic animations. I was delighted.

One of my first contributions was the use of voice-over announcers for some of their storytelling packages. When I returned to MLW, nearly all their packages used graphics and sound bites from the athletes and ringside announcers. A few dramatic lines, narrated by a talented announcer with a booming baritone, added another dimension and was a nice complement to the sound bites. It enhanced the excitement and drama of the stories the editors were telling.

I also wrote a lot of the copy for the packages and promos. Writing is also one of my passions. I was told that my assistance to one of the editors in postproduction had been "transformational." As compensation, I was given some shares of the company, in essence becoming one of their few minority owners. What an honor.

What was not transformational for my first nine months there was my influence in the production of the live show, no matter how optimistic I was. The first thing we did was fire the production company that had been producing their shows for two years and hire a new head of television production. The new guy hand-picked his own team of technicians, camera operators and audio engineers. We trusted him, having been promised a next-level look. It was anything but.

This new head of production was known in wrestling circles around the globe. He was genuinely nice to me and extremely knowledgeable, that much I can say. He bragged that he had numerous contacts with executives in high places and would help get us a TV deal.

It was all a façade. Later I would learn he had a reputation of overpromising and underdelivering, and that certainly proved to be the case at MLW. After we couldn't even make air on time in two of the three months he was in charge, he and his team of "experts" were gone.

What followed was potential that never fulfilled its promise. I convinced Court that we should use the same production truck and engineers that produce the shows for TNA. Though more expensive, we got a greatly reduced "friends and family" rate from my friend Eric Riley, the owner of MPS Productions. Court loved the idea, and I was delighted to be reunited with Riley and his team.

There was one major problem, however. Riley couldn't make the first show in New York City in December due to a prior commitment. Instead he assigned Matt Levine, his right-hand man, to be the engineer in charge for the first show. I had worked with Matt many times before and, like Eric, he was extremely talented. I was excited to show Court what this team could do.

Sadly, Matt's dad was hospitalized two days before the show in New York. Understandably, Matt wanted to stay with him, so Eric had to scramble to find yet another replacement just days before. I will not mention the name of this latest substitute because there isn't a good thing I can say about him professionally, at least as far as being the lead engineer and making sure everything worked from a technological standpoint.

The show was a debacle. There were numerous production breakdowns throughout the night, and the lead engineer tried frantically to fix a host of problems but found no solutions. I was frustrated beyond belief, and I sensed after just an hour that Court felt the same way and had already decided he would never use this team again. Who could blame him? I felt horrible. I felt I had let Court down, both personally and professionally. That was the lowest point of my tenure at MLW, even though I was not involved in the problems.

"If only" had reared its head again: If only Eric or Matt had been able to oversee the production of the show, everything would have been fine. It was decided later that week that we would go back to the original production company we fired when I first arrived.

The first show with the former production company was a bit rocky in the first hour; there is always a feeling-out process. But eventually we found our groove. In the months that followed, the live production was trending upwards. From lighting to audio, the shows finally looked and sounded professional. It was long overdue.

Major League Wrestling is a unique brand with a bold, brash and real feel, something that is hard to accomplish in this new age. The fighters fight hard, and the emotion is often real. It's creative and diverse, and I hope fans around the world will have more opportunities to immerse themselves in MLW in future.

During the show in December, and once again in February, Eric Bischoff agreed to appear on MLW television. It was great teaming up with him again. In the Monday Night Wars of the late nineties and early 2000s, he was the evil emperor of WCW *Nitro*, a fierce opponent trying to take WWE down, and he nearly succeeded. Under Bischoff's leadership the WCW beat WWE for eighty-three straight weeks and nearly put the company out of business. When he came to TNA in 2010 with Hulk Hogan, we connected from day one. I had nothing but pleasant experiences working with Eric at TNA from 2010 to 2014. He's a savvy businessman with an acute and brilliant mind.

Then one day in early April 2025, I received a phone call from him.

"I have an idea I want to run by you," he said.

The idea was Real American Freestyle Wrestling, also known as RAF. Hulk Hogan had been approached by two prominent executives from Left Lane Investments to be the face of this new venture. Having no knowledge of the production, Hogan had immediately called Bischoff, who'd then called me.

"Can you put together a budget of what it would cost to produce a live show this August?" he asked.

"I'd love to," I replied. "I have connections. We can do it at a good price, too."

"I'm not looking for a really good price. I'm looking for a really great production, something on the level of WWE and UFC."

"That I can do," I said. I could hear the joy in my own voice.

Eric explained his vision, and immediately I was stoked. Over the next couple of weeks I researched NCAA freestyle wrestling and was surprised how popular the live events were. They routinely sold out 18,000-seat arenas for their big events. Their fan base was passionate, but unlike the fans of WWE and AEW, they didn't make noise on social media.

What was missing from freestyle wrestling was a major streaming or cable network to televise the events. Eric's ambitious vision would present it in a way never seen before, and I was tasked with helping him and his partners at RAF create something big, something bold, something innovative. Suddenly, this became the biggest production of my career. To this day I cannot thank Eric enough for trusting me and allowing me to help him create something wonderful. What a full-circle moment: The former "evil emperor" from three decades earlier was now a genuine friend and ally.

I am a builder. And a believer. In every endeavor I have undertaken, I like to believe I helped make a difference. That is why I looked at my TNA termination as a blessing and not a burden.

It is also why I started my own ventures — as the CEO/founder of Bar Wisdom, an entertainment platform with its own line of apparel, and as the founder of a wrestling sitcom, *24 Station Street*, which I write, direct, produce and co-star in with a fellow entrepreneur, Jonathan Gordon.

Creation is what I crave. She's my midnight muse that all too often keeps me awake until the break of dawn. And I love it. At an age where I could soon retire if I choose, and look back on my achievements with pride, I choose to dwell in the now and the future and continually challenge myself. I awake eager every morning and look forward to the hidden gifts each day may bring.

This is not the end of my story. In many ways it is just the beginning. My dusk is really my dawn. My greatest achievement still patiently awaits.

I wouldn't want it any other way.

ACKNOWLEDGMENTS

The writing of this book has been a journey of my own past, and at times it's been difficult. But it's also been a mostly joyous ride that would not have been possible without the unwavering support and love of my inner circle. My heart is on these pages because of you.

To my father, Elias Joseph Sahadi, an author of thirty-one books — but more importantly, my mentor, my guide, my shining light in life. A man who never stopped believing in me when I had doubts about myself. "Poppa Lou" planted the seeds of possibility and belief in my heart and nurtured them with unconditional love. Poppa, my heart is your heart. It's you who made me the man I am today, and I am beyond grateful.

To my four siblings, especially my sister, Elizabeth, the epitome of love and positivity, a beacon of light in a world of darkness.

To my dearest friends, too many to mention, as well as the many strangers I encountered on my path of awareness and discovery. (Chris, Bryan, Jonathan, Tantra, Sarah and young Karlie — to name just a few.)

To the greatest bosses one could ever have: Scott D'Amore, Jeff Jarrett and now Eric Bischoff. They trusted me, gave my creativity room to breathe and treated me as a friend. Because of them, I never really "worked." Instead, I reveled in a world of ambition, co-creativity, and dreams turning into reality. In doing so, I danced with them in joy.

To my business partner, James Ontivero, a dear friend and kindred spirit, a brother with a heart of love and care that is rare.

To all those whose lives have touched mine in ways they will never know.

To my wonderful editor, Michael Holmes, who gently guided me throughout this process.

Finally, to the younger me, who ignored fear and dared to dream, defied conventions and danced with the outliers, the rebels, the ones who truly change the world. In doing so, I discovered the wings I needed to fly beyond horizons.

May we all find the courage to pursue our dreams and the strength to weather the storms.